Basic PowerPoint Exhibits

EasyTech Series

Basic PowerPoint Exhibits

Deanne C. Siemer

Frank D. Rothschild

National Institute for Trial Advocacy

Reproduction Permission
National Institute for Trial Advocacy
Notre Dame Law School
Notre Dame, IN 46556
(800) 225-6482   FAX (574) 271-8375
E-mail: nita.1@nd.edu   Web site: www.nita.org

Siemer, Deanne C., Frank D. Rothschild, *Basic PowerPoint Exhibits*
(NITA 2003)

ISBN 1-55681-823-8

CIP data is available upon request from Library of Congress.

TABLE OF CONTENTS

ACKNOWLEDGMENTS

The page design and editing on this book were done by Barb VanHolsbeke and Ashley Smith. The production of the book was coordinated by Shelly Goethals. The authors are also indebted to everyone who worked on the *PowerPoint for Litigators* book and the *PowerPoint 2002 for Litigators* book, from which the materials in this guide are drawn.

PowerPoint® is a registered trademark of Microsoft Corporation.

ABOUT THE AUTHORS

Deanne C. Siemer is a trial lawyer from Washington, D.C., who has specialized in commercial cases in federal and state courts, and who has tried large contracts, business torts, and patent cases using courtroom technology. She serves as a court-appointed arbitrator and mediator, teaches courses in trial practice and courtroom technology, and consults on case theory and presentation in trial cases.

Frank D. Rothschild has tried civil cases in private practice and criminal cases as a public defender and state prosecutor. He currently holds an appointment as a local court judge in Kauai, Hawaii, and serves professionally as a mediator and arbitrator. He teaches courses in trial practice and courtroom technology, provides training for judges and law firms, and consults on trial cases.

SEND US YOUR COMMENTS

We would like to hear from you! Visit the NITA Web site at www.nitastudent.org and tell us what you like about the book or what should be changed in the next edition. We are glad to get new slide ideas to be exchanged within the NITA family.

OTHER NITA TECHNOLOGY BOOKS

Effective Use of Technology, A Judge's Guide to Pretrial and Trial (Federal Judicial Center and NITA 2001). Distributed to all federal district judges, magistrate judges, and bankruptcy judges.

Effective Use of Technology, A Lawyer's Guide to Pretrial and Trial (NITA 2002) (with Donald Beskind and Anthony Bocchino). Companion to the *Judge's Guide* with additional material relevant to lawyers.

PowerPoint 2002 for Litigators (NITA 2002).

PowerPoint for Litigators (NITA 2000) (with Edward R. Stein and Samuel H. Solomon). Covers PowerPoint 2000 and PowerPoint 97 with three sample fact contexts for slides—criminal, business, and personal injury.

Guide for Teaching PowerPoint for Litigators (NITA 2000).

Corel Presentations for Litigators (NITA 2000). Provides all of the slide generation and presentation materials in the context of the Corel WordPerfect Office suite of software programs.

Easy Tech: Cases and Materials on Courtroom Technology (NITA 2001) (with Anthony Bocchino).

Demonstration: Presentation Technology in the Courtroom (NITA 2000) (with Samuel Solomon). Provides a script for demonstrating the use of the evidence camera, laptop computer, and telestrator in a trial setting.

INTRODUCTION

Electronic displays are an integral part of persuasive advocacy. PowerPoint is one of the relatively easy, inexpensive, widely available, and reliable software programs available to create the kinds of electronic displays that are useful at trial. This concise guide gives you the skills to prepare basic exhibits and illustrative aids.

This book focuses on PowerPoint 2002, which became available at the end of 2001. Lawyers who want to learn how to create electronic displays but have older versions of the software—PowerPoint 2000 or PowerPoint 97—should use *PowerPoint for Litigators* (NITA 2000) which was written specifically for those versions of the software.

Beginners and experienced computer users will find this material useful because it is focused specifically on designing and constructing the most common exhibits for use at trial. For more details on these and all other types of exhibits, see *PowerPoint 2002 for Litigators* (NITA 2002), which is a full-sized volume covering all of the elements of the software that are useful in litigation.

Creating slides is not difficult and does not require any extensive computer experience. The first chapter starts with turning on the computer, and goes from there. Each chapter tells you what you are going to do, describes in overview the steps necessary to get there, and guides you through the process one logical step at a time.

Taking completed PowerPoint displays into an opening statement, witness examination, or closing argument requires some modification of the lawyer's usual trial routine. These aspects are covered in *Effective Use of Courtroom Technology: A Lawyer's Guide to Pretrial and Trial* (NITA 2002), and *Easy Tech: Cases and Materials on Courtroom Technology* (NITA 2001).

Chapter 1: Setting Up to Use PowerPoint

This chapter covers what you need to know to set up PowerPoint for use in making trial exhibits and to work with PowerPoint's basic displays.

1.1 Setting up PowerPoint for trial slides

Setting up PowerPoint specifically for work on trial slides saves time and effort. Beginners can set up to work on trial slides and then read succeeding sections of this chapter that provide more detail on PowerPoint vocabulary and screen displays. Experienced users can read this section, then skip to chapter 2.

A. Your computer hardware and software.

Be sure that you have hardware and software that meets PowerPoint's minimum requirements. It is frustrating to work without the right tools.

1. Hardware.

PowerPoint does not require sophisticated computer equipment. You need—

- A laptop or other computer that has at least 128 MB of RAM and at least 10 MB of free storage space on the hard disk, which is needed to store the slides created in each chapter.

- A mouse plugged into the computer. This is useful even if the computer is a laptop.

- A CD drive in the computer or attached to it.

2. Software.

You need this software on your computer—

- Windows XP or any prior Windows operating system back to Windows 98 (Windows 2000, Windows ME, Windows 98). All of the illustrations in this book have been prepared on Windows XP. If you are using another Windows program, the colors and icons may look a little different, but the functions will be the same.

- PowerPoint 2002, which can be purchased as a stand-alone program or as part of the Office XP suite. If you have PowerPoint 2000 or PowerPoint 97, you should use the edition of this book, *PowerPoint for Litigators*, written specifically for those versions. It is available on the NITA Web site, www.nita.org.

B. Open the software.

To turn PowerPoint on, follow these steps.

1. Turn the computer on.

2. Click on the Start button. It is located at the very bottom-left corner of the screen. It looks like this if your computer is using the Windows XP operating system. A menu will appear above the Start button.

3. Click on the Programs option on this menu. Another menu will appear to the right listing all the programs available on your computer.

4. Move the mouse pointer to the Microsoft PowerPoint option on this programs menu. Click on this option.

The opening screen will appear. It looks like the illustration on page 4.

C. Check the key parts of the display.

You should check the basic parts of the screen display to be sure all the tools you need for building litigation slides are on the screen. This saves time later on. If any are missing or out of place, sections 1.3 and 1.4 describe how to retrieve and move them.

> The default screen display (which appears until you tell the software to do something else) is set up to make a bullet list slide, as this is the most common type of work that users want to do with PowerPoint. The "Click to add title" instruction has to do with that type of slide. Ignore it for now and finish setting up your computer. Bullet list slides are covered in chapter 3.

1. Windows bars.

The top blue bar, the Title Bar, at the left tells you what program is currently active and at the right displays the standard Windows minimize/maximize/close buttons. The bottom blue bar, the Task Bar, at the left has the START button; across the middle shows what programs are running; and at the right usually displays the current time and other icons indicating shortcuts to software available on the computer.

Title Bar

Microsoft PowerPoint - [Presentation1]

Menu Bar

File Edit View Insert Format Tools Slide Show

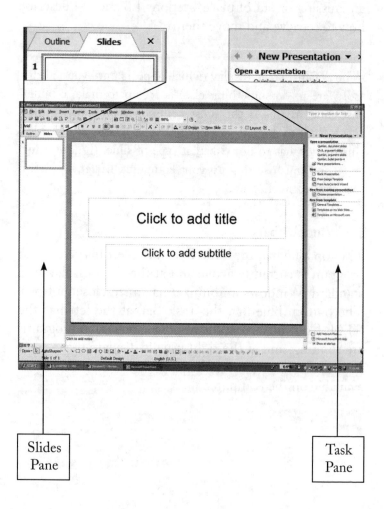

Slides Pane

Task Pane

Two other elements, the Menu Bar that sits at the top of the screen just under the blue Title Bar, and the Status Bar that sits at the bottom of the screen just above the blue Task bar, are also standard Windows bars that appear with every software program that is run using the Windows operating system.

2. PowerPoint panes.

The panes are panels that appear at the left edge and right edge of the screen containing tools arranged in ways to help you work more efficiently. The panes are shown in the illustration on page 4.

If the panes are not showing on your screen, go to section 1.3 which describes how to restore them. If they are narrower than the panes shown in the illustration, go to section 1.3 which describes how to adjust them.

3. PowerPoint toolbars.

The basic screen display also has four toolbars—the Standard and Formatting Toolbars at the top, and the Drawing and Picture Toolbars at the bottom. Toolbars can be moved and changed. You need to check to be sure all are displayed in the locations shown in the illustration on the page 6.

The Standard and Formatting Toolbars should be displayed on two rows under the Menu Bar. The Drawing and Picture Toolbars should be displayed on one row above the Status Bar.

Standard Toolbar

Formatting Toolbar

The Standard, Formatting, and Drawing Toolbars are shown here in segments (in order to fit the illustration on the page), although they appear as a single row on the screen.

View Bar

Drawing Toolbar

Picture Toolbar

If these toolbars are missing or out of place, section 1.4 describes how to restore and move them.

In addition, PowerPoint has one bar—the View Bar—located in the lower-left corner (usually just above the Drawing Toolbar) that is basic to the PowerPoint software and does not move or change.

If there are additional toolbars displayed (other than the four shown in the illustration), close them. Section 1.4 describes how to do that. PowerPoint has fifteen toolbars, but other than the basic four all are for very specialized purposes.

D. Adjust the toolbars and buttons.

If the computer and software have been used by others, it is usually a good idea to adjust the toolbars. This makes it easier to follow the directions in this book because the illustrations will look like your screen display.

The adjustments are quickly and easily done—

1. Put the Standard and Formatting Toolbars on separate rows.

The Standard Toolbar and the Formatting Toolbar can sit on the same row at the top of the screen, but if they do, there is not room for all their buttons. This is not a problem, because there is a method to add and remove buttons (see section 1.4 below), but it can be annoying not to have the buttons you need displayed at all times. If you put them on separate rows, they can be displayed with all their buttons.

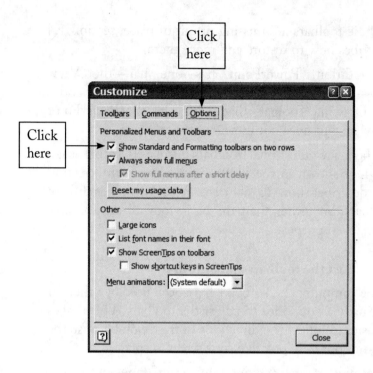

This is an example of what PowerPoint calls a "dialog box." It is a screen display that contains a number of related options.

Select an option by clicking on the small boxes where there are check marks. Clicking on an empty box will produce a check mark and activate that option. Clicking on a box with a check mark will delete the check mark and deactivate that option.

Tabs at the top of a dialog box are controls. Clicking on a tab will change the display within the dialog box to a different set of options.

The other settings shown in this illustration of the Customize dialog box are also useful for working on exhibits.

To do this—

    a. Go to the Menu Bar (located just under the blue Title Bar at the top of the screen).

    b. Click on the Tools button. A drop-down menu will appear.

    c. Click on the Customize option on the menu. A dialog box will appear showing a number of choices for customizing the way the PowerPoint screen works.

    d. Click on the Options tab at the top of the dialog box. The display will look like the illustration on page 8.

    e. Look at the small checkbox that says "Show Standard and Formatting toolbars on two rows." It should be checked. If not, click on it to check it.

    f. Click on the Close button at the bottom of the dialog box. The toolbars should now be on two rows, with the Standard Toolbar on top and the Formatting Toolbar underneath.

2. Reset each toolbar and display all buttons.

Buttons can be moved around on a toolbar and, if your computer and software have been used by someone else, it is a good idea to reset the toolbars to their standard configuration.

    a. Reset the toolbar.

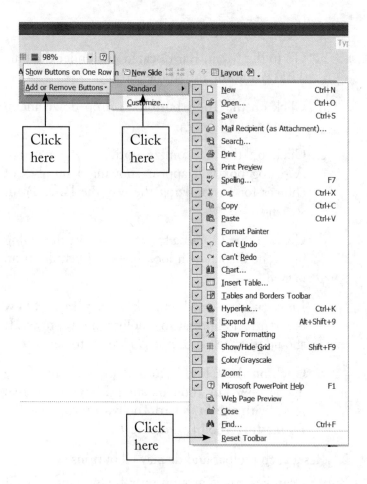

These are examples of what PowerPoint calls "menus." A menu is a list of options. To activate an option, click on it. To deactivate an option that is currently activated, click on it. A check mark in a box in front of an option indicates that it is active.

i.   Go to the Standard Toolbar.

ii.   Look at the very end of the toolbar. There will be a small down arrow. Click on it.

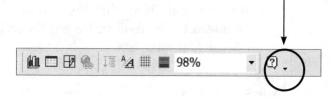

A small two-item menu will appear. It looks like the illustration on page 10.

iii. Click on the Add or Remove Buttons option. Another small two-item menu will appear.

iv. Click on the Standard option. A dialog box showing all of the buttons on the Standard Toolbar will appear. If there is a check mark in the small box in front of the name of the button, then the button is currently displayed on the toolbar.

v.   Go to the very bottom of the list. Click on the listing that says Reset Toolbar. This will put the buttons in a standard order and display all of the most commonly used buttons. Some buttons that are used infrequently will not be checked.

b. Display all the toolbar's buttons.

i.   Follow the steps under (a) above to get to the dialog box.

ii. Move your mouse pointer over the first name of a button that is unchecked. The name of the button and its icon will be highlighted. Click on it. A check mark will appear indicating that the button has been added to the toolbar. Repeat for each unchecked button.

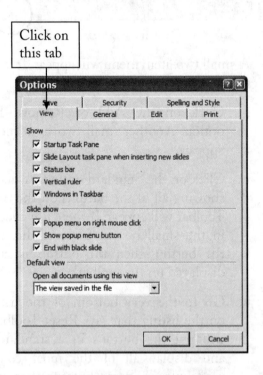

The other settings controlled by the Options dialog box—the tabs labeled Save, Security, Spelling and Style, General, Edit, and Print—do not directly affect the methods for building PowerPoint slides described in this book, but it is a good idea to check them (click on each tab in turn) at the outset just to be aware of your system's default settings.

E. Adjust other settings.

PowerPoint allows you to specify how the features displayed on the screen will appear or act. It is frustrating to try to do some PowerPoint operation only to have the computer not cooperate because a setting tells it to do something else.

These settings are very easy to adjust, and the directions and illustrations in later chapters assume that the settings are as recommended in this section.

1. Bring up the Options dialog box.

Most of the convenient options for litigation slides are listed on a display that is illustrated on page 12 and that you can find this way—

   a. Go to the Menu Bar. This is the bar right under the blue bar at the top of the screen.

   b. Click on the Tools button. A drop-down menu will appear.

   c. Click on the Options button. A dialog box will appear.

2. Activate the View tab settings.

   a. Click on the View tab at the top of the dialog box. After you click on the View tab, the display looks like the illustration on page 12.

   b. Check all the boxes. Do this by moving your mouse pointer over each small square box and clicking on it.

   c. Click on the OK button at the bottom of the dialog box.

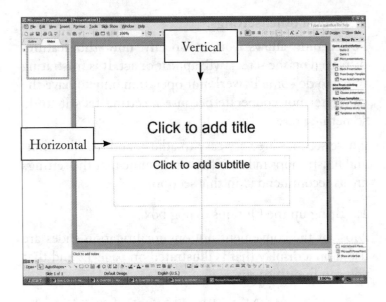

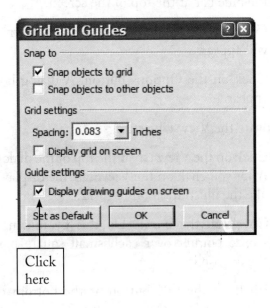

F. Display the Guides.

Some of the common designs for litigation slides involve lining up a number of objects or text boxes evenly and neatly with regard for margins, centering, and other aspects of slide layout. This is sometimes difficult to do by eye, and is particularly important if your slides are going to be projected onto an 8-foot projection screen where all flaws will be made much larger.

PowerPoint has a vertical Guide and a horizontal Guide that, when turned on, appear as dotted lines on your screen when you are building slides. These dotted lines help you get things centered on the slide or lined up along a particular axis. They are not visible when you present your slide show.

When you add the Guides, the screen display looks like the illustration on page 14.

To display the Guides—

1. Go to the Menu bar.

2. Click on the View button. A drop-down menu will appear.

3. Click on the Grids and Guides option. A dialog box will appear. It looks like the illustration on page 14.

4. Check the small box labeled "Display drawing guides on screen" by clicking on it. A check mark will appear.

5. Click on the OK button at the bottom of the dialog box. The Guides will appear on the screen.

Centering objects: The Guides are at dead center when they first appear on the screen. This means that the top- and bottom-middle handles on an object can be lined up with the vertical Guide to center them between the left and right edges of the slide, and the left and right middle handles on an object can be lined up with the horizontal Guide to center them between the top and bottom margins of the slide.

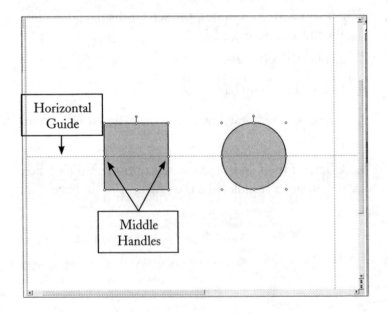

In this example, the objects have been lined up with the horizontal Guide. In this position, they are equidistant from the top and bottom of the slide.

Measuring distance: The Guides are movable, and can be used to measure the distance from top and bottom or from left and right to get objects placed evenly on a slide. The horizontal Guide can be dragged up and down, and the vertical Guide can be dragged from side to side. Position the mouse pointer over the Guide, hold down the mouse button, and drag the Guide. As they are dragged, the Guides display small numbers where the mouse pointer is located showing the distance from center in decimals.

1.2 Basic vocabulary and alternative controls

Explanations about PowerPoint require a number of common terms associated with the Windows operating system. PowerPoint also uses specialized terms that are virtually inescapable in working with trial exhibits. For the most part, technical terms have been stripped away to make the text easier to follow. The basic technical terms are listed here.

A. Windows vocabulary.

Cursor: The blinking vertical line that appears on the screen indicating where text will go when typing begins. (Also sometimes called the "insertion pointer" because it indicates where something will be inserted.)

Mouse pointer: The shape that moves around the screen as you move the mouse. The mouse pointer changes shape (one arrow, I-beam, two-arrow, four-arrow, cross) as you set up to perform different functions. The shape of the mouse pointer tells you what function the system is prepared to perform.

Click on [something]: Place the mouse pointer in the designated area, press the left mouse button once, and release it. Occasionally, the software requires a right click (press the right mouse button and release). When a right click is required, the text will specifically point that out. Otherwise "click on" always means the left mouse button.

Button: Areas on the screen, typically located on a toolbar and defined by a word label or icon, where you can click to activate a PowerPoint function.

Minimize/maximize: The Windows software always presents three control buttons in the upper-right corner of the screen.

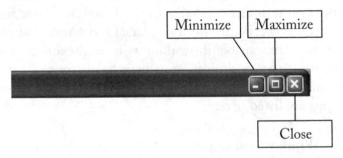

Windows can make the current window (for example, displaying PowerPoint) disappear leaving only an icon representing this window on the blue Task Bar along the bottom of the screen. This is the "minimize" function. When you want that window back, you can go back to the Task Bar, click on the icon, and it will reappear. Windows will also make the current window increase in size so that it takes up the entire screen (if it does not do that already). This is the "maximize" function. The third button in this group closes the program altogether.

Default: Windows and the software running under it will do things in a certain way if they are not told to do something else. The "default" option is what the software will choose if left to its own devices.

B. PowerPoint vocabulary

Slide: This is a single visual aid, constructed with PowerPoint, which can be displayed on a computer monitor, or through a digital projector, on a projection screen.

Slide show: This is a collection of slides intended for a specific purpose or a presentation.

View: This is a screen display. PowerPoint does three basic things: create slides, organize individual slides into slide shows, and display slide shows. It has three Views, one for each of these purposes. The Normal View is used to create slides, the Slide Sorter View is used to organize slide shows, and the Slide Show View is used to display finished slide shows.

Object: This term includes shapes (such as a box, rectangle, or circle), lines, documents, photographs, and diagrams placed on a slide as a part of carrying out the design of the slide. Objects can be moved, resized, aligned with other objects, filled with text, colored, given borders, and animated in order to deliver the slide's intended message more effectively.

Activate (an object or a slide): PowerPoint manages the operations that go into preparing a slide by requiring you to designate where you want to work next. You activate the area where you will be working by highlighting it (in the case of text) or clicking on it (in the case of boxes or other objects).

C. PowerPoint's alternative ways of doing things.

PowerPoint often provides two, three, or even four alternate ways of doing the same thing. In this book, the descriptions and illustrations focus on the easiest and most generally applicable method for most beginners.

Many of the recommended controls are screen controls where you click on a button on the screen to initiate an action. A few are keyboard controls where you hold down the CTRL key and press another key to initiate an action. Occasionally a right click mouse control is useful.

For mouse controls, the left mouse button produces action; the right mouse button produces options—usually a menu from which you can choose what you want to do.

1.3   PowerPoint Panes

The panes are long vertical displays of controls along the right and left side of the screen. These are clusters of working tools to help get slides constructed and edited more efficiently. (See illustration on page 4.)

The left side of the screen has the Slides/Outline Pane (usually called the Slides Pane because the most frequently used panel displays thumbnails of all the slides in the slide show you are working on). The right side of the screen has the Task Pane. This is a housing for ten separate panes, each of which presents specialized controls for particular tasks.

A. Add a pane that is missing.

Each of the main panes can be restored to the screen display at any time.

1. Slides Pane.

    a. Go to the Menu Bar.

b. Click on the View button. A drop-down menu will appear.

c. Click on the Normal option at the top of the menu. This will restore all of the panes usually present in the Normal View, including the Slides Pane.

d. Click on the Slides tab at the top of the pane.

2. Task Pane.

a. Go to the Menu Bar.

b. Click on the View button.

c. Click on the Task Pane option. This will restore the Task Pane.

B. Adjust the width of a pane.

1. Move the mouse pointer over the border of the pane that is next to the main area in the center of the screen. As the mouse pointer hovers over the border, it will turn to a two-arrow shape.

2. Hold down the mouse button and drag the border so that the pane is wider or narrower.

When the pane is narrowed, the content remains the same. Use the scroll bar at the right side of the pane to scroll down to content on the longer, narrower display.

C. Close a pane that is not needed.

Each pane has a small Close button at the top right, marked with an X. Click on this Close button and the pane will disappear. This is sometimes useful if you need more work room on the screen for the slide.

1.4 PowerPoint toolbars

This section provides a brief description of the toolbars provided by the software. Buttons on toolbars are often easier to remember than the alternative controls, and many of the operations described in the book work off of toolbars.

A. Add a toolbar that is missing.

PowerPoint often loads with the Standard, Formatting, and Drawing toolbars but without the important Picture Toolbar. To add this or any other toolbar—

1. Go to the Menu Bar.

2. Click on the View button. A drop-down menu will appear.

3. Click on the Toolbars option. A dialog box listing all of the available toolbars will appear. The ones displayed on the screen will have a check mark.

4. To add a toolbar, click on its checkbox, a check mark will appear, and the toolbar will appear on the screen.

B. Move a toolbar to a new position.

A toolbar may show up on the right or left side of the screen (instead of at the top or bottom), in a floating position in a random place on the screen, or above or below another toolbar. You can move any toolbar to a different position.

Each toolbar has a move handle that allows you to drag the toolbar to a new location. The handle is located at the far left of the toolbar, just in front of the first button. It is a small dashed vertical bar that looks like this enlarged version.

1. Move the mouse pointer over the toolbar move handle.

2. Hold down the left mouse button.

3. Drag the toolbar to the position where you want it to be located. Let up on the left mouse button, and the toolbar should lock into place.

C. Close a toolbar that is not needed.

Use the method for adding toolbars, and uncheck the box in front of its name. The toolbar will disappear from the screen display.

1.5 PowerPoint pointers, borders, and handles

PowerPoint has standard ways of telling you about the functions or features that you are about to use or signaling what set of functions is available.

A. Pointers.

The cursor and the mouse pointer perform different tasks, and the instructions in this book will often direct you to use one or the other.

1. Cursor.

The cursor appears only when the software expects you to be typing something—letters, numbers, or symbols. When you start typing, the first letter appears at the cursor's location. The cursor appears in only one way. It is always a blinking vertical line. (The cursor always blinks; the mouse pointer never does.) You can move the cursor to a new location in three ways. The first is to put your mouse pointer at the desired spot and click on the left mouse button to position the cursor. The second is to use the keyboard's arrow keys. The third is to use the keyboard's tab key.

2. Mouse pointers.

The mouse pointer is used for functions other than typing—activating buttons, menus, options, and dialog box choices for example. The pointer can take a number of shapes, as shown below, depending on what the software is being asked to do. It may be a single-headed arrow, a double-headed arrow (pointing up and down, sideways, or crosswise), a four-point arrow, an I-beam, an hourglass, a hand, a cross, and other shapes.

Common Mouse Pointer Shapes

▷	One-arrow	Selects buttons and menu options
I	I-beam	Appears when you are where you can type
↔	Two-arrow	Drags handles to change the shape of boxes
✥	Four-arrow	Drags things to another place
+	Cross	Indicates where shapes will be placed
⌗	Crop	Changes the shape of pictures

PowerPoint has an extensive built-in help system. If you want to know about a particular button, put the mouse pointer over it, hold down the SHIFT key on the keyboard, and press the F1 key at the top of the keyboard. A question mark will appear. Click again and a text explanation will appear.

For more information go to the Menu Bar, click on the HELP button, and click on the Microsoft PowerPoint Help option. Microsoft provides updates to PowerPoint 2002 on its Office Update Web site. To get there, go to the Menu Bar, click on the Help button, click on the Office updates on the Web option.

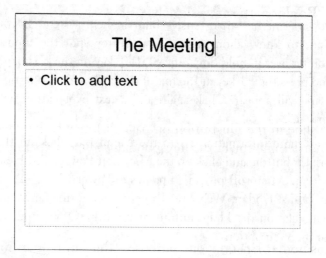

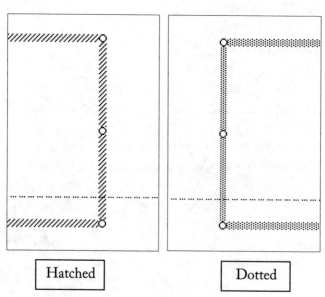

Hatched

Dotted

B. Border patterns as signals.

Sometimes you need to look closely at the borders of specialized boxes (or other objects) on the screen because the pattern on the border signals what can be done with the box as long as the current border is showing. The border for the title box (which says "The Meeting" on the slide in the illustration on page 26) may be hatched or dotted, and the box will respond differently depending on which it is.

1.   Hatched border.

A hatched border is made up of small diagonal lines. This border has only one purpose. You can type in the box or edit what you have typed.

2.   Dotted border.

A dotted border is made up of many small dots. When this border is active, you can work on text (edit, color, change typeface and type size), change fill and line colors, move, resize, and copy the box. Any text within the box is automatically activated and ready to be worked on. It does not have to be highlighted in order to use text buttons (font, font color, bold, italic, underline, shadow, and other text effects). However, all the text in the box will be changed in the same way.

3.   Switch from one border to the other.

Put the mouse pointer anywhere on the border and click on it. The border will change. In some cases for instance, if you are working in a box with a dotted border and you start to type in additional words, PowerPoint will switch borders automatically.

C. Handles.

A handle is a control that allows you to move part or all of an object. PowerPoint provides three sets of handles: sizing handles, rotate handles, and perspective handles. The sizing and rotate handles are most useful for litigation purposes.

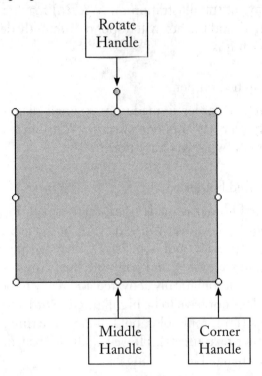

1. Sizing handles.

The sizing handles are embedded in the border of a box or other shape. You can see the small circles in the illustrations of box borders above. These are sizing handles. You use handles by putting your mouse pointer over them and (after the mouse pointer changes to a two-arrow shape indicating it is ready to move the object), holding down the mouse button, and dragging the handle.

§1.5

a. Middle handles.

The handles in the middle of the top and bottom margins change height. The handles in the middle of the side margins change width.

b. Corner handles.

The handles in the corner change height and width at the same time to keep the object proportionally the same although its absolute size is increased or decreased.

2. Rotate handle.

The rotate handle is a small round green handle extending from the top of an object. It allows you to turn the object around—either moving clockwise or counterclockwise.

Chapter 2: Basic Moves in PowerPoint

Five moves will provide a good starting point for most kinds of slides—create a blank slide, color the background, use a text box, duplicate a slide, and delete a slide. This chapter covers these basics in the context of creating a "black slide" that is used multiple times in every slide show prepared for use at trial.

When you are using your computer in a courtroom, you want it to wait silently, with nothing visible on the screen, until you are ready to go. At that instant, you want the slide show to come alive with the first slide without any distraction between the point you are making orally and the first point you make visually. This is accomplished by using a black slide as the first slide in the show.

The black slide shows nothing on the screen except a small light-colored square in the lower-right corner. The rest of the screen appears blank although, in reality, the computer is projecting the black slide. As long as the little square is on the screen, you know the computer is operating and ready to go to the next slide, which will be the opening slide in the show. If the little square disappears, you know you have trouble.

Black slides are also used in the middle of a slide show. A black slide effectively "blanks" the screen. When the screen is dark, jurors' attention is focused on the lawyer. Similarly, at the end of a slide show, perhaps near the end of your closing argument, you want the screen to show no image at all, so you can move to the concluding arguments in your oral presentation with the focus solely on you.

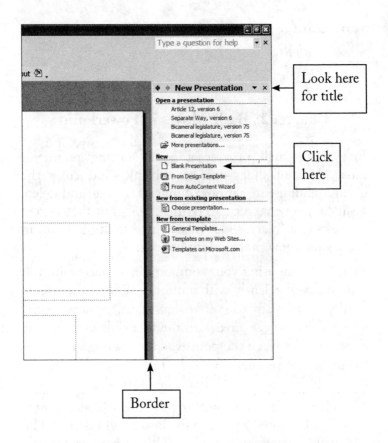

If the title of the pane is truncated, you can adjust the width of the pane by dragging its border. See instructions in section 1.3 above.

If PowerPoint is not already running on your computer when you start to work, turn it on. Follow the instructions in section 1.1.

2.1   Create a blank slide

A blank slide is the starting point for many kinds of litigation slides. PowerPoint has a large number of preformatted layouts, but most do not work well in a courtroom. The blank slide will permit you to tailor all of the details for the courtroom situation.

A. Check to be sure the Task Pane is showing.

The Task Pane is a generic name for the panel located along the right side of the screen. (See illustration on page 4.) If the Task Pane is not there, restore it. (See discussion in section 1.3.)

B. Go to the New Presentation Pane.

The Task Pane houses the New Presentation Pane. The title of the pane is at the top of the panel, as shown in the illustration on page 32. If the New Presentation title is not showing at the top of the pane, click on the arrow key immediately to the right of the title. A drop-down menu will appear. Click on the New Presentation option.

The New Presentation Pane has four sets of options for starting your work.

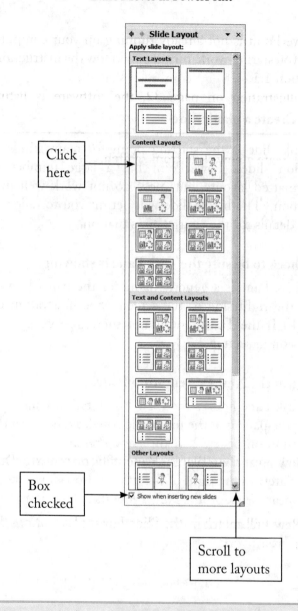

Click here

Box checked

Scroll to more layouts

The small box at the bottom-left corner labeled "Show when inserting new slides" should be checked. If it is not, click to check it. This brings the Slide Layout Pane to the screen automatically when the New Slide button is used.

You can—

- Open a slide show that already exists on your computer and continue that work. (In the illustration on page 32, the software is listing several existing files. If you have done no PowerPoint work, yours will be blank).

- Create a new slide from scratch.

- Pick a slide from an existing presentation to start a new slide show.

- Start with a template that comes with the software.

A template is a basic design for a slide, complete with colors and typeface choices provided by the software. Most templates provided by the software or Web sites are geared toward business and sales presentations.

For trial work, you will likely use only the first three options 1, 2, or 3. Commercial templates usually do not work well in the courtroom.

C. Open a Blank Presentation.

1. Click on the Blank Presentation option. (See illustration on page 32.)

When you click on the Blank Presentation option, the Task Pane will switch to the Slide Layout Pane. Now the Task Pane looks like the illustration on page 34.

It displays four category headings: text layouts, content layouts, text and content layouts, and other layouts.

2. Click on the Blank Slide option.

The display in the middle of your screen will change from the default option (title and subtitle) to a blank screen.

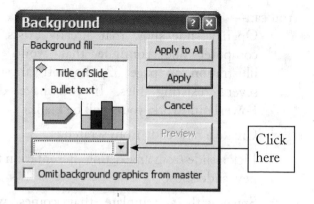

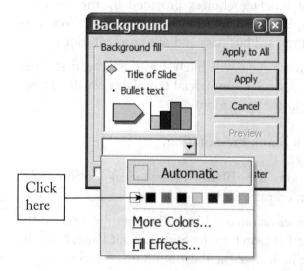

Do not use the Apply to All button. That will use black as the background for every slide in the slide show.

---

2. Click on the Blank Slide option.

The display in the middle of your screen will change from the default option (title and subtitle) to a blank screen.

2.2   Color a slide

◆

The "background" of a slide is the area of the slide behind anything (like text or shapes) that you put on the slide. The term background usually refers to color.

A. Open the Background dialog box.

1. Go to the Menu Bar.

2. Click on the Format button. A drop-down menu will appear.

3. Click on the Background option. The Background dialog box appears in the middle of the slide on which you are working. It looks like the first illustration on page 36.

B. Designate the color.

1. Click on the small down arrow next to the box indicating the current color choice. (Note: the blank slide has a white background, so the box shows a white color.) A second dialog box appears. It looks like the second illustration on page 36

2. Click on the small box representing black. The Background dialog box will now show your choice—a black background—so you can check to see if it is what you want.

3. Click on the Apply button on the Background dialog box. Your slide will now be colored black.

2.3 Use a text box

◆

A PowerPoint slide consists of a background (covered in section 2.2 above) and design elements put on that background. Everything that is put on the slide is called an "object." In PowerPoint terms, a "box" is a square or rectangle that is one kind of object. A "text box" is one kind of box that has been specially designed for text to be typed into it if words are to be put on the slide. The text box is one of the principal tools in working with litigation slides.

This section covers how to put a text box on a slide and then color, resize, rotate, move, duplicate, and delete it.

A. Put a text box on a slide.

1. Activate the text box control.

    a. Go to the Drawing Toolbar at the bottom of the screen.

 b. Click on the Text Box button. It looks like the illustration to the left, with lines representing text on it. This creates a text box that can be placed anywhere on the slide.

2. Place the text box onto the slide.

    a. Move your mouse pointer toward the lower-right corner of the slide.

    b. Click once at the location you have chosen. A small text box appears on your slide with a blinking cursor in the middle. It has a hatched border with handles embedded in the border. It looks like this.

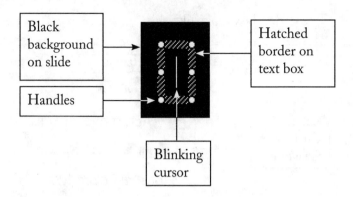

B. Color a box.

In this case, it is useful to add a white (or gray, to be more subtle) color to the box. This will allow the small text box to show up well against the black background, and also to be unobtrusive on the screen. Color within a box (or other object) is called "fill color." (The box must be active (border and handles showing) in order to color it.)

1. Open the Fill Color Dialog box.

    a. Go to the Drawing Toolbar.

    b. Click on the down arrow just to the right of the Fill Color button. This button looks like the illustration to the left, with a paint can pouring out color on it. A dialog box will appear.

The dialog box looks like this.

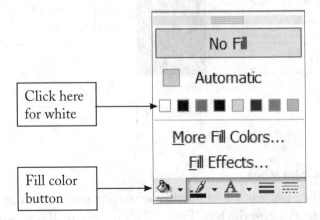

The dialog box appears immediately above the Drawing Toolbar where the Fill Color button is located.

When you choose a fill color, a small bar on the Fill Color button shows that choice. To add the same fill color to other objects, just click on the Fill Color button, which eliminates the extra step of going to the dialog box.

2. Choose the color.

Click on the small box representing white. The text box will turn white. It now looks like this.

C. Resize a box.

You can make the box longer with the middle handles that show up as small circles in the left and right borders of the box. The box must be active (border and handles showing) in order to resize it.

1. Decide which handle to use.

Position your mouse pointer over one of the handles. The mouse pointer shape will change from an arrow with one point to an arrow with two points, one at each end.

2. Drag the handle.

    a. Hold down the left mouse button.

    b. Drag the handle outward to increase the size of the box, or inward to decrease the size of the box. Use a box that is small enough not to be noticed readily by the jury but that is easily visible to you.

    c. Release the left mouse button when the box is the desired size.

D. Rotate a box.

Just for practice, turn the box 90 degrees so that it rests on its side. The box must be active (border and handles showing) in order to rotate it.

1. Locate the rotate handle on the box.

The rotate handle is a small green dot sitting just above the top of the box. If the green dot is not showing, enlarge the text box a little more, and it will appear.

2. Drag the handle.

    a. Move your mouse pointer to the green dot and hover there until the mouse pointer changes shape and becomes a circle.

b. Hold the left mouse button down and drag the rotate handle in a clockwise direction. The box will turn in the direction you drag the handle.

E. Move a box.

On a black slide, the white marker box should be unobtrusive, so you may want to locate the indicator box closer to the margin of the slide, or to the left or right of the location where you initially put it. There are three ways to move a box—across a relatively large space, across a relatively small space, and across a very small space.

1. Large moves.

a. Move your mouse pointer over the border of the box. The mouse pointer will change to a four-arrow shape. (See illustration in section 1.5.)

b. Look at the border of the box. The border indicates what operations can be performed with the box. The box will move when the *dotted* border is showing. It will not move when the hatched border is showing. (See illustrations of these borders in section 1.5.)

c. If the hatched border is showing, click on it. This will cause it to switch from the hatched border to the dotted border.

d. With the mouse pointer over the border, and the dotted border showing, hold down the left mouse button and drag the box to a new location. Let up on the mouse button when the box is where you want it.

2. Small moves.

a. Activate the box so that the *dotted* border is showing, as above. The controls to make small moves will not work if the hatched border is showing.

b. Press one of the directional ARROW keys on the keyboard. This moves the box in relatively small increments in the direction indicated by the arrow.

If you hold down the ARROW key, the object will keep moving in small increments.

3. Very small moves.

a. Activate the box so that the *dotted* border is showing, as above.

b. Hold down the CTRL key on the keyboard, and press one of the directional arrow keys on the keyboard. This moves the box in very small increments in the direction indicated by the arrow.

F. Duplicate a box.

Just for practice, duplicate the small white marker box.

1. Activate the *dotted* border.

a. Move your mouse pointer over the border of the box.

b. Click to switch to the dotted border if necessary. (The controls to duplicate a box will not work if the hatched border is showing.)

2. Use CTRL + D.

Hold down the CTRL key on the keyboard and press the D key. A duplicate box will appear just below and to the right of the original box.

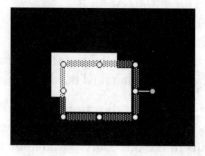

The CTRL + D keys will duplicate any object—a photo, document, rectangle, line, or oval.

3. Move the duplicate box to a new location. (See step E above.)

G. Delete a box.

Just for practice, delete the duplicate box that you have created.

1. Activate the *dotted* border.

   a. Move your mouse pointer over the border of the box to be deleted.

   b. Click to switch to the dotted border if necessary. (The controls to delete a box will not work if the hatched border is showing.)

2. Press the DELETE key on the keyboard. The duplicate box will disappear.

2.4   Duplicate a slide

It is often useful to create duplicates of slides because the duplicate will contain all of the formatting and design work you have done on the original. This saves considerable time.

A. Activate the thumbnail of the slide.

1. Go to the Slides Pane.

This is the panel on the left edge of the screen that shows thumbnails (or miniature versions) of your slides as you create them. It is shown in the illustration on page 46.

2. Click on the thumbnail of the black slide. A blue border will appear around the thumbnail indicating that it is "active."

B. Use CTRL + D.

Hold down the CTRL key on your keyboard, and press the D key at the same time. A duplicate slide will appear on your Slides Pane.

The blue border is now around this slide, as it is the one that is active. You now have two black slides—one for the beginning of the show and one for the first break in the show where you will be using only an oral presentation and not slides. The next slides that you create will go between these two slides. The screen will look like the illustration on page 46.

Thumbnails on
the Slides Pane

If the Slides Pane is not displayed, restore it (see section 1.3). If the Slides Pane is displayed but no thumbnails are showing, click on the tab labeled "Slides" at the top of the pane.

2.5   Delete a slide

You may want to take a slide out of a slide show if you have decided that it does not work or is not needed.

Delete one of the black slides just for practice—

A. Activate the thumbnail.

1. Go to the Slides Pane (the panel on the left edge, shown in the illustration above).

2. Click on the thumbnail of the slide to be deleted. A blue border will appear around the slide indicating that it is active.

B. Use the DELETE key on the keyboard. Press the delete key once. The slide will disappear from the Slides Pane and has been deleted from the slide show.

2.6 Save your work

It is very important to save your work often. Glitches happen and can cause you to lose slides or entire slide shows if they have not been saved.

A. Open the Save As dialog box.

1. Go to the Standard Toolbar.

 2. Click on the Save button. The button looks like the illustration to the left, with a floppy disk (which used to be the principal means of saving files) on it.

When you save your work on a particular slide show for the first time, PowerPoint delivers the Save As dialog box that asks you to name the file. When you save this file on subsequent occasions, the Save button operates automatically. The dialog box looks something like this, depending on how your computer is set up and what folders it contains.

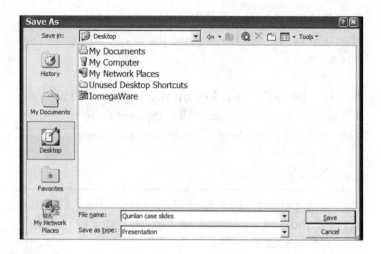

B. Create a folder in which to save your slides.

1. Go to the Save In box at the top of the dialog box.

When you first go to the Save As dialog box, the Save In box usually displays the location called "Desktop."

That is the most general location that your computer has. It is the very first screen that appears when you turn your computer on. You can accept this location, or change it. It is not a good idea to store all your files on the desktop because that screen will become cluttered.

2. Select the "My Documents" folder.

The Save As dialog box offers you a general alternative, which is the "My Documents" folder. That is a general storage place, and a good choice when you are starting out because the "My Documents" choice appears on the screen in almost every view, so you can always get back there.

Click on the "My Documents" name in the window on the dialog box (or click on the button called "My Documents" in the panel on the left side of the dialog box). "My Documents" will now appear in the Save In box at the top of the dialog box.

3. Create a new folder within the "My Documents" folder.

A folder is a software device that organizes files. Some folders are already created when you start up the computer for the first time. The "My Documents" folder is this kind of ready-made folder. (Depending on which operating system you are using, other ready-made folders may appear such as "My Pictures," "My Music," and "My Broadcasts.")

Any folder can hold just files, or it can also hold a number of other folders if you want to organize your files further. To create a folder for your slide shows, within your "My Documents" folder, do this—

a. Go to the toolbar at the top of the Save As dialog box. It looks like this.

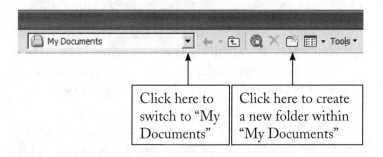

b. Click on the New Folder button. A small dialog box will appear.

c. Type the name for the folder in the dialog box.

d. Click on the OK button. The name of the new folder will now be in the "Save In" box on the toolbar.

Now you can save the file containing the photo, and it will be put in the new folder.

When you click on the "My Documents" folder, it will display the new folder.

C. Designate a name for the file.

    a. Go to the File Name box at the bottom left.

    b. Choose a short name for this slide show.

    c. Type the name into the File Name box.

D. Designate a file type for the file.

The file "type" is the format which the software uses to store the file. There are several available formats each of which serves a special purpose.

    a. Below the File Name box, you will see the Save As Type box.

    b. "Presentation" is the choice that should be showing. That is the right choice for working with your slides. If something else is showing, click on the arrow at the right side of the box to display a drop-down menu and pick the Presentation option.

E. Save the file.

Click on the Save button at the lower right. This completes the process.

It is important to save your work early and often during the process of constructing slides. A lot of time-consuming work can be lost to computer crashes.

2.7   Close, exit, and reopen the program

◆

A. Close the file.

1. Go to the Menu Bar.

2. Click on the File button. A drop-down menu will appear.

3. Click on the Close option.

4. If you have made any changes since you last saved the file, PowerPoint will ask you if you want to save these changes before exiting the program. Choose yes to save the file, or no to discard the changes.

B. Exit the program.

1. Go to the Menu Bar.

2. Click on the File button. A drop-down menu will appear.

3. Click on the Exit option at the very bottom of the menu.

C. Reopen the program.

This is the same as shown in section 1.1(B).

D. Reopen the file.

1. Go to the Task Pane. (Illustration in section 1.1.) If the Task Pane is not showing on the right edge of the screen, restore it. (See section 1.3.)

2. Go to the New Presentation Pane. (If another pane is showing, click on the arrow to the right of the pane

name, and a drop-down menu will appear. Click on the New Presentation Pane option.)

3.   At the top, under the heading "Open A Presentation" there should be the name of the file that you saved. Click on the name of the file. The first slide in the file will appear on the screen.

When you use PowerPoint 2002 for the first time (and several times thereafter), the software will display a box asking you to register. This can be done by telephone or Internet connection. Registration can be completed at any time, but the program can be opened only fifty times without registering.

> For instructions on how to run the slide show once you have created it, see section 7.1.

Chapter 3: Bullet Point Lists

A basic list of points, without any artistic effort at all, can increase the power of your advocacy. A list helps get across the logic of your presentation and the facts that support your themes. It illustrates how one point is related to other points and makes the listener feel comfortable because the structure of the presentation is apparent.

A good bullet point list has a short title at the top and four to six evenly spaced one-line statements underneath the title. All of the points are directly related to the title. Each statement conveys only one thought. The text is stripped of all extraneous words. All that remains are the minimum words necessary to make the point. The oral presentation does the rest.

The Meeting

- Four hours in Kane's study
- Talked about selling business
- Reviewed his alternatives
- Kane wanted to sell business
- Quinlan in the business of selling

The skills outlined in this chapter will allow you to begin using polished visuals right away.

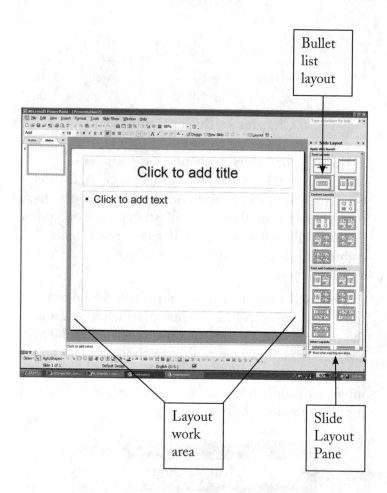

Bullet list layout

Layout work area

Slide Layout Pane

The layout work area in the middle has the directions "Click to add title" and "Click to add text" on it. PowerPoint assumes that you will want to control the title separately from the bullet point list. The title typically will be a larger type size, for example, and may have a different color scheme to set it off from the bullet points below it.

3.1   Create a basic bullet point list

You can construct a functional bullet point list from start to finish by opening the bullet list layout, adding a title, and adding bullet points. Working on a good list of points helps hone your own thinking about your oral presentation.

A. Open the bullet list layout.

There are a number of ways to lay out a bullet list. PowerPoint has a preformatted layout for bullet lists that works well for trial exhibits. The easiest way to get to this layout is as follows—

1.   Go to the Formatting Toolbar.

 2. Click on the New Slide button. This will display the Slide Layout Pane.

The New Slide button usually displays the bullet list layout as a default. If it does not, click on the bullet list layout on the Slide Layout Pane. This layout has two text boxes—one for a title and one for the bullet points. The screen will look like the illustration on page 54.

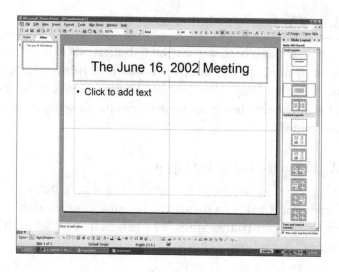

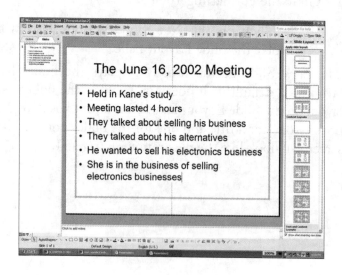

B. Add a title.

1. Pick a title that summarizes a topic that you would cover in an opening statement. In the example on page 56, the lawyer has decided to make several points about a particular meeting that is important to the case.

2. Move your mouse pointer anywhere inside the top box (where it says "Click to add title"). Click on the left mouse button. The pointer is now an I-beam shape. (See illustration in section 1.5.) Clicking inside a text box "activates" the box, and a border appears around the edge of the box. (See illustration in section 1.5.)

3. Type the title in the title box. See, for example, the title in the illustration on page 56.

The text in a title box is centered automatically. The vertical Guide shows the center position. (See discussion of Guides in section 1.1(F).)

4. Move your mouse pointer anywhere outside the title box. The pointer now changes back to the one-arrow shape. Click on the left mouse button. Now you can see how your slide looks thus far.

C. Add bullet points.

1. Pick the points you would make about the topic that is contained in the title.

2. Move your mouse pointer anywhere in the lower box where it says "Click to add text." Click the left mouse button. The mouse pointer is an I-beam. A light bullet point appears to the left of your pointer.

3. Start typing. PowerPoint is now working like a word processor. See, for example, the bullet points in the illustration on page 56.

The text in a bullet list layout is aligned on the left margin.

4. Hit the ENTER key on your keyboard when you finish a bullet point. PowerPoint will start the next bullet. If you make mistakes, just use the BACKSPACE key on your keyboard, and type the text over again. The next section will show you how to edit the text.

5. Do not hit the ENTER key after creating the last bullet point.

6. Click anywhere outside the text box to see your slide in finished form. The first draft of your slide is done.

D. Save your work. (Standard Toolbar, Save button.)

Your first draft will probably need improvement as this slide does. We all tend to start off with points that are too wordy and that need to be pared down.

3.2   Edit a basic list

Editing text on slides is very similar to editing sentences in word processing work. If you use Microsoft Word, the commands in PowerPoint are the same. If you use another word processor, the commands are very similar. After you have typed text into a box on the slide, you can delete unnecessary words or entire bullet points, add words or new bullet points, reorder the bullet points, and create subordinate points.

Striking extraneous words keeps you focused on the essentials. Rearranging the order in which your points are made lets you examine alternative ways to persuade. Examples are shown in the illustration on page 62.

A. Delete unnecessary words.

1. Activate the title box by clicking anywhere on the text in the box. Decide whether any of the words in the current title can be deleted.

2. Delete words in the title box using any one of three convenient methods.

 a. *Backspace key*: Move the mouse pointer to a location at the end of the word to be deleted. Click to position the cursor there. Press the BACKSPACE key on the keyboard to delete each letter moving from right to left.

 b. *Delete key*: Move the mouse pointer to the beginning of the word to be deleted. Click to position the cursor there. Press the DELETE key on the keyboard to delete each letter moving from left to right.

 c. *Highlight*: Highlight the words to be deleted by placing your mouse pointer at the beginning, holding down the left mouse button, and dragging the mouse to the end of the words. Then release the mouse button. The text will be highlighted and the title box looks like this.

The June 16, 2002 Meeting

If there were only one meeting at issue in the case, you might elect to pare down the title by deleting the date.

Press the DELETE key. Now the title looks like this.

The Meeting

B. Delete entire bullet points.

1. With the text box containing the bullet list active, highlight all of the text of the bullet point plus one space past the last letter.

2. Press the DELETE key on your keyboard. Even though you did not highlight the bullet itself, when PowerPoint deletes all of the text associated with a bullet, it also deletes the bullet.

C. Add words.

1. With the text box containing the bullet list active, place your mouse pointer on the line of text at the place where you want to add a word. Click your left mouse button. The cursor will be blinking at this point.

2. Type the word or words to be added.

D. Add new bullet points.

1. To add a new bullet point, put the mouse pointer at the end of the bullet point just prior to the new point.

2. Click to place the cursor at that point.

3. Press the ENTER key on the keyboard. A new bullet point will appear, and you can type your text after it.

In most cases as you add bullet points, PowerPoint will automatically reduce the type size if there is insufficient space on your slide for the new material. You can go back to your original type size by increasing the size of the bullet box. See section 3.3.

E. Reorder bullet points.

1. To move a bullet point up in the order on the slide, put the cursor anywhere in the text to be moved, go to the Formatting Toolbar, and click on the Up button.

2. To move a bullet point down in the order on the slide, put the cursor anywhere in the text to be moved, go to the Formatting Toolbar, and click on the Down button.

Editing bullet list slides is often a serial process in which improvements are made, which in turn suggest further improvements as illustrated on page 62.

Bullet Point Lists

BEFORE	AFTER

BEFORE	AFTER
• Held in Kane's study • Meeting lasted 4 hours • They talked about selling his business • They talked about his alternatives • He wanted to sell his electronics business • She is in the business of selling electronics businesses	• Kane's study • 4 hours • talked about selling business • talked about his alternatives • He wanted to sell business • She is in the business of selling
• Kane's study • 4 hours • talked about selling business • talked about his alternatives • He wanted to sell business • She is in the business of selling	• Kane's study • talked about selling business • talked about his alternatives • He wanted to sell business • She is in the business of selling
• Kane's study • talked about selling business • talked about his alternatives • He wanted to sell business • She is in the business of selling	• Four hours in Kane's study • Talked about selling business • Reviewed his alternatives • Kane wanted to sell business • Quinlan in the business of selling

• Four hours in Kane's study
• Talked about selling business
• Reviewed his alternatives
• Kane wanted to sell business
• Quinlan in the business of selling
	• Four hours in Kane's study
	  – Talked about selling business
	  – Reviewed his alternatives
	• Kane wanted to sell business
	• Quinlan in the business of selling

F. Create subordinate points.

 1. To create a new subordinate point, first create a new bullet point, then go to the Formatting Toolbar and click on the Increase Indent button. The shape of the bullet will change and the new subordinate bullet will be indented. Type your text as you would in making a bullet point.

Alternatively, with the cursor at the beginning of the new bullet point, press the TAB key on the keyboard to indent the bullet point.

2. To make an existing bullet point into a subordinate point, put the cursor immediately in front of the bullet point, then click on the Increase Indent button. PowerPoint will automatically change the size and shape of the bullet when a point is subordinated. The size of the type is also reduced.

 3. To reverse a subordinate point (and send it back to the margin as a regular bullet point), put the cursor immediately in front of the text of the bullet point to be reversed, and click on the Decrease Indent button.

Alternatively, with the cursor at the beginning of the new bullet point, hold down the SHIFT key on the keyboard, and press the TAB key on the keyboard for the same result.

G. Save your work.

3.3 Enhance the appearance of a basic list

This section includes five useful ways to make slides easier to comprehend—use a line border around the box, resize and move the box, adjust the text or the bullets, and add color or shadow. These techniques can be used alone or in combination.

As you dress up your slides, you will come to appreciate the enormous range of tools included in the software. Some of the more extreme of these (not covered in this section) are not applicable to courtroom use unless you have had a lot of experience using PowerPoint slides in trials and have found particular things that work well for you. See *PowerPoint 2002 for Litigators* (NITA 2002) for more of these techniques.

A. Put a line border around the box.

Because the border that PowerPoint puts around a box will disappear when you move to another box or something else on the slide (and will come back when you activate the box again), it is usually helpful to put a line around each box, in effect a more permanent border. This lets you see the outline of the box while you are working on other areas of the slide. When you finish designing the slide and you decide that you don't want the line around the box, it is easy to remove. The slide with lines around the box looks like this.

The Meeting

- Four hours in Kane's study
- Talked about selling business
- Reviewed his alternatives
- Kane wanted to sell business
- Quinlan in the business of selling

§3.3

To add lines around a box—

1. Activate the box.

2. Activate the dotted border if it is not already showing. (Move the mouse pointer over the border until the four-arrow shape shows, then click the left mouse button.)

3. Go to the Drawing Toolbar.

4. Click on the Line Style button. (There are three style buttons together.)

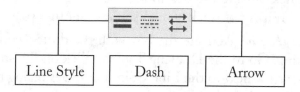

A dialog box will appear. It shows lines of various thicknesses, and looks like this.

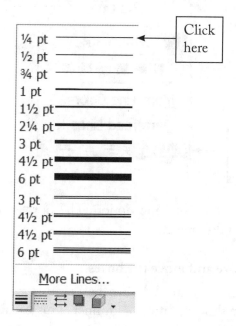

When you use lines for trial slides, follow the principle of "least visual difference." Use the smallest width of line that will get the point across. That way, the lines will not distract from the overall message of the slide.

5. Click on the ¼-point option. A line will appear around all four sides of the box.

When you pick a line style (size) for a particular purpose, it is a good idea to stay with that selection throughout your slides.

6. Click outside the box to see the line that is now in place. If it is not thick enough, choose another size.

Delete the line: Activate the box with the dotted border showing. Go to the Drawing Toolbar, click on the small down arrow next to the Line Color button. A dialog box will appear. It looks like this.

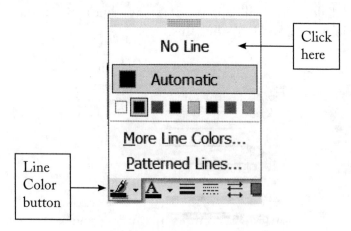

Click on the No Line option. The border (which is a line) will disappear.

B. Resize and move the boxes.

Any box on your slide can be made larger or smaller, taller or shorter, fatter or thinner. This capability helps with many design tasks. For example, sometimes as you juggle the words in your slide, you realize that you need to make the text box a little wider so your bullet points can fit on one line, or a little taller so the spacing between your bullet points can be increased for ease of reading.

1. Resize the box.

There are two ways to make a box bigger or smaller. You can resize by moving a single border or you can resize proportionally by moving all borders at once. The single border method is useful for making a box narrower, and the proportional method is useful for creating more space around a box on all sides.

a. Resize by moving a single border.

   i. Locate the single border handle you want to use. Single border handles are small circles in the middle of each border. They look like this.

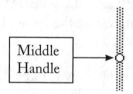

   ii. Move the mouse pointer to a position over the handle. In order to drag a handle, the mouse pointer must be showing a two-arrow shape. You may have to move the mouse pointer back and forth a bit to get the two-arrow shape to appear.

   iii. With the two-arrow mouse pointer over the handle, hold down the left mouse button and drag the handle in the direction you want the border to move. When you reach the right spot, release the mouse button.

b. Resize proportionally (all sides).

   i.   Locate the proportional handle you want to use. Proportional handles are small circles at the four corners of each text box. They make the box larger (if dragged outward) or smaller (if dragged inward) while maintaining the proportions of the box.

   ii. Move the mouse pointer to a position over the handle. In order to drag these handles, the mouse pointer must be showing a two-arrow shape.

   iii. With the two-arrow mouse pointer over the handle, hold down the left mouse button and drag the handle in the direction you want to change the overall size of the box. When you reach the right spot, release the mouse button

2. Move an entire box.

You can move the entire box up, down, and sideways to achieve better balance in the slide design.

a. Move the mouse pointer over any part of any border that is not a handle. In order to move the entire box up, down, or sideways, the mouse pointer must be showing a four-arrow shape. You may have to move the mouse pointer back and forth a bit to get the four-arrow shape to appear.

b. Hold the left mouse button down and drag the box in the direction you want it to move. When you reach the right spot, release the mouse button.

C. Adjust the shape, size, and emphasis of the text.

These factors determine how readable the text is when presented in the courtroom, and how easy it will be for jurors to grasp your points readily.

The Meeting

- Four hours in Kane's study
  - Talked about selling business
  - Reviewed his alternatives

- Kane wanted to sell business

- Quinlan in the business of selling

In the example above, the typeface (shape and size) has been adjusted, boldface has been used for emphasis, and the spacing has been adjusted (see section E below). To explore the options with text, do this—

1. Change the shape (typeface) of the text.

The typeface that you use for the words on your slides has a very substantial effect on how readable they are.

The typeface for a bulleted list should be one of the clean sans serif typefaces. **Arial** is a good choice. **Tahoma** is another good choice.

With your slide on the screen—

    a. Change the title.

i. Activate the title box by clicking anywhere on the text within it.

ii. Click on the border if necessary to switch to the *dotted* border. This border automatically activates all of the text within the box so that you can make any change to the text as a whole without highlighting.

iii. Go to the Formatting Toolbar. The name of the currently active typeface is displayed in the white box at the left side of the toolbar.

iv. Put your mouse pointer on the small arrow immediately to the right of the box listing the typeface, and click on it. A drop-down menu will show you a list of the available typefaces. Click on an option on the menu, and the typeface on the title will be changed.

  b. Change the bullet points

i. Activate the bullet box.

ii. Follow steps ii through iv above.

2. Change the size of the text.

The type sizes for the title and text should be proportional to each other and readable at the distance your display screen will be from the judge and jury. The title is usually set in a size larger than the text. The choice depends on the display screen you will be using.

Consider these combinations for title and text sizes:

Title	Text
44 point	36 point
40 point	36 point
36 point	32 point
32 point	28 point

a. Change the title.

    i. Activate the title box.

    ii. Make sure the *dotted* border is showing.

    iii. Go to the Formatting Toolbar. The size of the currently active typeface is displayed in the small box immediately to the right of the name of the typeface.

    iv. Click on one of the Font Size buttons. Click on the large letter A to make the type size increase one size, and click on the small letter A to make the type size decrease one size.

b. Change the bullet points.

    i. Activate the bullet box.

    ii. Make sure the *dotted* border is showing.

    iii. Use the Font Size buttons as above.

When making a series of bullet point slides for use at trial, consistency is key. Once you pick a combination of titles and text sizes, it is best to stick with that combination throughout your series.

D. Add emphasis to the text.

There are two ways to add emphasis. You can add emphasis to everything in the box, or you can add emphasis to selected words within the box.

Everything in the box: Activate the box containing the text to which emphasis will be added. Make sure the dotted border is showing. (See illustration at section 1.5.)

One or several words in the box: Highlight the text to be changed. (Put the mouse pointer at one end, hold down the left mouse button, and drag the highlight to the other end.) Once highlighted, only those words will be changed by what you do next to add emphasis. The rest of the text in the box will be unaffected.

B   1. *Bold*: Go to the Formatting Toolbar. Click on the Bold button. All of the text will change to boldface. When the boldface feature is on, the Bold button will be highlighted. To delete the boldface, click on the Bold button again.

I   2. *Italic*: Go to the Formatting Toolbar. Click on the Italic button. When the italic feature is on, the Italic button will be highlighted. To delete the italic, click on the Italic button again. Italic should be used sparingly on trial slides because it is more difficult to read.

<u>U</u>   3. *Underline*: Go to the Formatting Toolbar. Click on the Underline button. When the underline feature is on, the Underline button will be highlighted. To delete the underline, click on the Underline button again. Although underlining is useful in some contexts, for litigation slides it is generally much less effective than alternative methods for adding emphasis.

4. *Shadow*: Go to the Formatting Toolbar. Click on the Shadow button. To delete shadow, click on the Shadow button again. Shadow sometimes helps set off a title box or helps make the text in a title box distinct from the text in the bullet box. However, shadow can also make the slide confusing, so it should be used carefully.

E. Adjust bullet point spacing.

1. Adjust the spacing between the bullet points.

    a. Activate the bullet box with the *dotted* border showing.

    b. Go to the Formatting Toolbar.

    c. Click on the Increase Paragraph Spacing or Decrease Paragraph Spacing button.

With each click, the spacing between the bullet points will increase or decrease.

2. Adjust the spacing between the bullet points and the top of the bullet list box. (This is useful if you have a line border around the box and the first bullet point is too close to or far away from the border.)

    a. Activate the bullet box with the *hatched* border showing.

    b. Go to the Formatting Toolbar.

    c. Click on the Increase Paragraph Spacing or Decrease Paragraph Spacing button.

With each click the bullet points will move farther away from (Increase) or closer to (Decrease) the line border.

Bullet tab

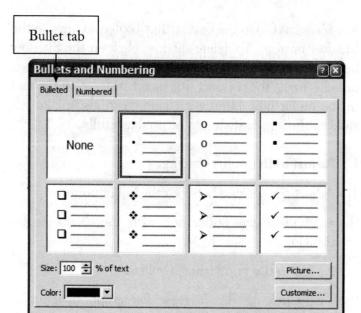

Number tab

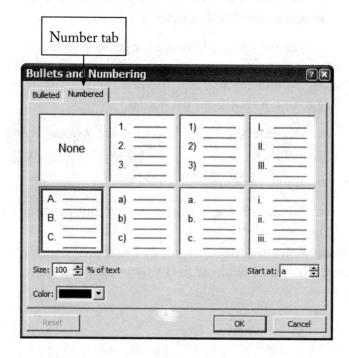

F. Adjust the shape and style of the bullets.

The PowerPoint bullet list layout comes with circular black bullets that are matched in style and size to the typeface you have chosen and that have a standard spacing between bullet and text. These are excellent choices for most courtroom uses. If you decide to change these standard settings, be sure you have a good reason.

1. Adjust the shape of the bullet.

PowerPoint provides seven standard options for the shape of bullets (and also an option to remove the bullets altogether).

a. Activate the text box containing the bullets you want to change.

b. Make sure the dotted border is showing. (Click on the border to switch to it if it is not showing.)

c. Go to the Menu Bar.

d. Click on the Format button. A drop-down menu will appear.

e. Click on the Bullets and Numbering option. A dialog box will appear.

f. Click on the Bulleted tab at the top of the box (if it is not already showing). The display in the dialog box looks like the illustration on page 74. The default option (which is round black bullets) will be highlighted.

g. Click on the square that shows the shape you would like for your bullets.

h. Click on the OK button at the bottom of the box. The bullets on your slide will change to the shape you have selected.

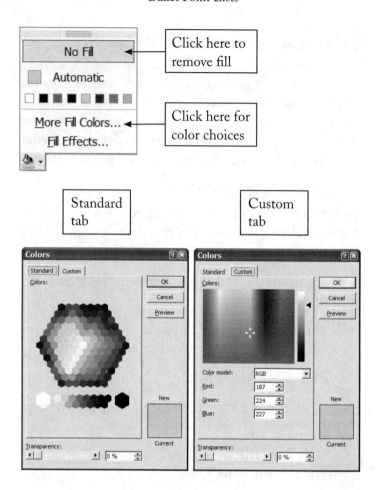

The software provides two ways to get exactly the colors you need. The Standard Color set shows color polygons, with a set of gray polygons below. Put your mouse cursor on the color you want and click on it. The Custom Color set provides a wide range of hues plus the option to mix your own by specifying the precise amount of red, green, and blue for the mix. The New/Current box compares what you have on the slide now with your proposed change. The Preview button allows you to see what your selection would look like; the OK button implements the choices.

2. Change the style of the bullets to numbers or letters.

    a. With the dotted border showing, go to the Menu Bar.

    b. Click on the Format button. A drop-down menu will appear.

    c. Click on the Bullets and Numbering option. A dialog box will appear.

    d. Click on the Numbered tab at the top of the dialog box. This will switch the display from the options for bullets to the options for numbers and letters.

    e. Click on the square that contains the number or letter option you need.

    f. Click on the OK button at the bottom of the dialog box.

G. Add color to the elements of the slide.

This section covers color for all the parts of the slide—the background, fill, lines, text, and bullets. It is a good practice to add the color to all the elements at one time, so that your thinking about color focuses on how one color relates to another.

1. Color the background of the slide. See section 2.2.

Delete background color: If you decide to return to a no-color background, follow the same directions and switch to a white color.

2. Color the interior (fill) of a box.

a. Activate the box. The controls for fill color will work with either type of border showing (hatched or dotted).

b. Go to the Drawing Toolbar.

 c. Click on the small down arrow to the right of the Fill Color button. A dialog box will appear. It looks like the illustration at the top of page 76.

The Fill Color button has a small bar underneath the icon. This displays the current color that you have selected. If you want this color again, you can just click on the button and it will appear. There is no need to go to the dialog boxes.

d. If the color you want is shown in the row of small colored boxes, click on it. If not, click on the More Fill Colors option. The standard Colors dialog box appears. (See illustration on page 76.)

e. Click on the color you want.

f. Click on the OK button in the upper-right corner of the dialog box. The color will be added to the interior of the text box.

Delete the fill: If you decide you want to delete the fill color, go to the Drawing Toolbar. Click on the down arrow next to the Fill Color button. A dialog box will appear. (Illustration on page 76.) Click on the No Fill option at the top of the box. The fill color will disappear.

3. Color the lines around a box.

a. Activate the box that has the lines you wish to color. The Line Color feature works with either border (hatched or dotted).

b. Go to the Drawing Toolbar.

c. Click on the small down arrow to the right of the Line Color button. A dialog box will appear. It is similar to the illustration at the top of page 76.

The Line Color button has a small bar underneath the icon. This displays the current color that you have selected. If you want this color again, you can just click on the button and it will appear. There is no need to go to the dialog boxes.

d. Click on the color you want to add if it appears in one of the small boxes displayed on the dialog box. The color of the lines on your slide will change.

e. If the color you want is not displayed, click on the More Line Colors option. The Colors dialog box will appear. Click on the color you want, and click on the OK button at the top right of this dialog box. The color of the lines on your slide will change.

Delete the line color (return to black): If you decide you want to delete the line color, go to the Drawing Toolbar. Click on the down arrow next to the Line Color button. A dialog box will appear. Click on the black color button at the top of the box. The line color will disappear and the line will be black.

4. Color the text in a box.

a. Activate the box by clicking on it.

b. Make sure the dotted border is showing (if you want the color to apply to all of the text) or highlight the particular text to which color is to be added.

c. Go to the Drawing Toolbar.

d. Click on the small arrow to the right of the Font Color button. A dialog box will appear. It is similar to the illustration on Page 76.

The Font Color button has a small bar underneath the icon. This displays the current color that you have selected. If you want this color again, you can just click on the button and it will appear. There is no need to go to the dialog boxes.

> e. If the color you want is in the dialog box, click on it. Otherwise click on the More Colors button. The lettering on your slide will change color.

Return to black: If you do not like the shade that you picked when you see the display on the screen, go back through these steps again and pick another one or return to black.

5. Color the bullets.

If you change the color of the text in a box containing bullets, PowerPoint will automatically change the color of the bullets to match the color of the text. If you want the bullets to be a color different from the text, do this—

> a. Activate the box containing the bullet text.

> b. Highlight the text of the bullet points for which you wish to change the bullet color. (If you intend to change the color of only one bullet in a set, put the cursor anywhere in the text of that bullet.)

> c. Go to the Menu Bar.

> d. Click on the Format button. A drop-down menu will appear.

> e. Click on the Bullets and Numbering option. A dialog box will appear.

f. Click on the Bulleted tab at the top of the dialog box. The display in the dialog box will look like the illustration on page 74.

g. Go to the Color box. Click on the small down arrow next to the box (usually black) displaying the color of the current bullets. A dialog box will appear.

h. Click on the color you want. One option that works well is to use the same color for the bullets and the line around the box.

i. Click on the OK button in the lower-right corner of the dialog box. The bullets will change to the color you have chosen.

j. If the color you want is not in the initial dialog box, click on the More Colors button at the bottom of the dialog box, and the Colors dialog box will appear with many more choices. Click on the color you want. Then click on the OK button at top of the dialog box.

Return to black: If you do not like the shade that you picked when you see the display on the screen, go back through these steps again and pick another one or return to black.

H. Save your work. Go to the Standard Toolbar. Click on the Save button.

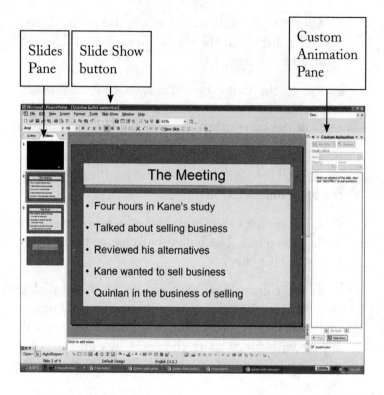

The Custom Animation screen is set up so that you can record your answers to three basic questions.

· Should the text move in some way as it comes onto the screen?

· Should the text move while it is on the screen?

· Should the text move while it is going off the screen?

The answers for bullet point slides are different from the answers for other kinds of slides.

3.4   Animate a basic list

Animation is a name for the set of controls that allows you to reveal each bullet on your slide one by one and to add motion so that each bullet appears on the screen from a particular direction. This section covers only the controls necessary to animate these slides for their normal use in opening statements and direct examination.

This section explains how to set up to add animation to bullet point lists; how to animate the title and the individual bullet points; then how to preview the animation and make changes if necessary.

The fundamental purpose of animation when dealing with bullet point slides is to keep your audience from reading ahead. You want them to concentrate on the point about which you are speaking.

A. Set up to add animations.

1. Put your first bullet point slide on the screen.

    a. Go to the Slides Pane on the left side of the screen. (See illustration on page 82.)

    b. Find the thumbnail of the first bullet point slide and click on it. This will bring the slide to the screen.

2. Display the Custom Animation Pane on the right side of the screen. (See illustration on page 82.)

    a. Go to the Menu Bar.

    b. Click on the Slide Show button. A drop-down menu will appear.

    c. Click on the Custom Animation option. The Custom Animation Pane will appear.

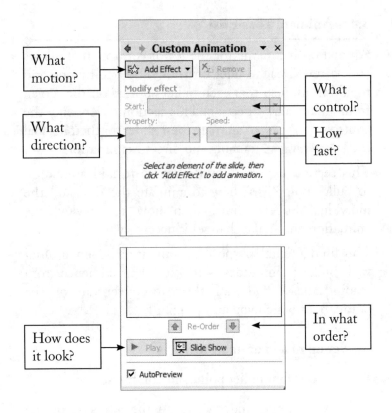

Because the Custom Animation Pane contains a lot of detailed information, normally you will want to have it at full size. See discussion at section 1.3 on how to expand the size of the pane.

d. There should be a check mark in the AutoPreview box at the bottom of the Custom Animation Pane. This activates the preview function so you can see how the animation effects that you choose actually function on your slide. If the check mark is not there, click on the box to add it.

B. Animate the title.

1.   Select the Entrance effect. An "Entrance effect" is the motion by which the text (or an object) arrives on the slide.

a. Activate the title box by clicking on the text in the box.

b. Go to the Custom Animation Pane.

c. Click on the button at the top that says "Add Effect." A menu will appear listing four types of effects. It looks like this.

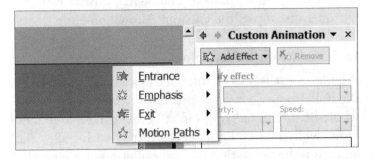

d. Click on the Entrance option. Another menu will appear listing the available Entrance effects.

The "Appear" and "Wipe" effects work well with text and are appropriate for bullet slides. Most of the other Entrance effects are designed for objects such as boxes and other shapes rather than text.

The effects that are listed on this menu, and the order in which they are listed, can change. PowerPoint attempts to put within easy reach the effects you use the most. Click on "More Effects" at the bottom of the menu to see the rest of the list.

e. Click on the Appear option.

The automatic preview will show this action. However, because the "Appear" option just makes the title appear all at once, the preview is very brief. This animation is now attached to the title box, and the screen display changes to reflect this.

2. Select any other (Emphasis, Motion Path, Exit) effects for the title.

Bullet point slides generally do not make use of effects other than the Entrance effect.

3. *To remove an animation,* click on the listing for the particular animation on the Custom Animation Pane. It will then be highlighted in blue. Click on the Remove button at the top of the Custom Animation Pane.

C. Animate the bullet points.

A bullet point list can be animated as a whole by activating the bullet point box and applying the animation to the whole box. Alternatively, bullet points can be animated individually by highlighting the text of each bullet and attaching the animation to each bullet point. Generally, animating the entire box is sufficient.

1. Select the Entrance effect.

   a. Activate the bullet point box.

   b. Go to the Custom Animation Pane.

   c. Click on the Add Effect button at the top. A short menu will appear listing the four principal categories of effects. (See illustration on page 85.)

   d. Click on the Entrance option. Another menu will appear listing the first seven to nine types of Entrance effects. (There are fifty-two of these altogether. You can see them by clicking on the More Effects option.)

   e. Click on the Wipe option. (If the Wipe option is not showing on the menu when it initially appears, click on the More Effects button and scroll down until you find it.) The top of the Custom Animation

Pane now shows the default settings for this option. It looks like the illustration on page 88.

The software will automatically play a preview of this option on your slide so that you can see what it does. You will see that the default direction for the Wipe option is from bottom to top, and the default speed for the Wipe option is Very Fast. The Bottom to Top direction is virtually never used in litigation slides, and the Very Fast speed option has to be moderated for courtroom presentations.

2.   Consider whether to change the Start control.

The Start control has three alternatives: Start on a mouse click; start with previous; and start after previous. The default is Start on a mouse click. This is generally the best for bullet lists.

The "Start with previous" option brings two or more items to the screen together. The "Start after previous" option automates the action so that one item follows the next with no mouse click.

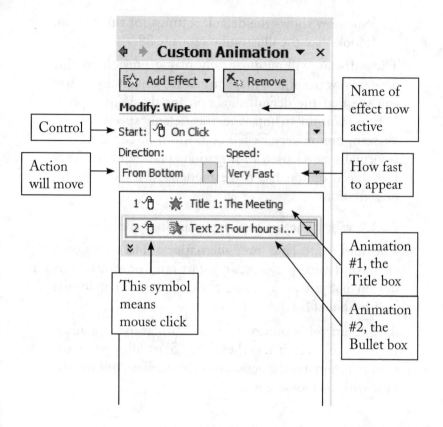

3. Change the Direction control so the text moves from left to right.

   a. Go to the Direction control. The box currently says "From Bottom."

   b. Click on the down arrow to the right of the box. This will display four choices (From Bottom, From Left, From Right, From Top).

   c. Click on the From Left option. This rolls the text out from left to right the way people normally read English. The AutoPreview will show you this action on your slide.

4. Change the speed to Fast.

    a. Go to the Speed control. The box currently says "Very Fast."

    b. Click on the down arrow to the right of the box. This will display five choices (Very Slow, Slow, Medium, Fast, Very Fast).

    c. Click on the Fast option. This rolls the text out fairly quickly. Fast and Medium are the two most suitable options for bullet point slides. The AutoPreview will show you this action on your slide.

5. Display the individual bullet items in the bullet point box.

    a. Go to the small down arrow just below the listing for the bullet point box (which has the number 2 at the left edge).

    b. Click on it. This will display each of the individual animations within the bullet point box. There should be one for each bullet point. The Custom Animation Pane now looks like the illustration on page 90.

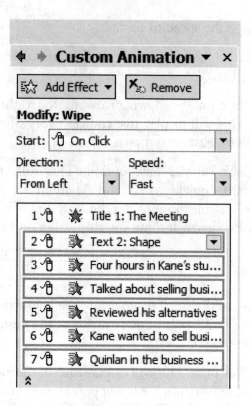

There are now seven mouse clicks for this slide. The slide will start with just the background showing.

1. The first click brings up the entire title box.

2. The second click will bring up (rolling from left to right) the shape of the text box with nothing in it.

3. The third click will bring up (rolling from left to right) the first bullet point.

4. The fourth click will bring up the second bullet point.

5. The fifth click will bring up the third bullet point.

6. The sixth click will bring up the fourth bullet point.

7. The seventh click will bring up the fifth and last bullet point.

6. Select any other (Emphasis, Motion Path, Exit) effects for the bullet points.

Bullet point slides generally do not make use of effects other than the Entrance effect.

To delete an animation: Click on the numbered item on the Custom Animation Pane representing the part of the animation that you would like to delete. A blue border will appear. Click on the Remove button at the top of the Custom Animation Pane.

D. Preview the animation.

You can preview the animation at any point in the process, but it is always a good idea to do a preview when you are finished or nearly finished with a slide.

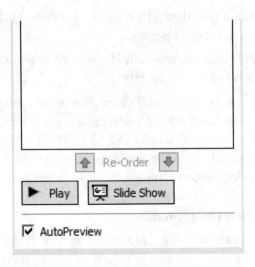

The bottom of the Custom Animation Pane provides two ways (in addition to the AutoPreview) to preview the animation you have applied to the slide to be sure that it will work properly. You can either "Play" the animation with your working screen in place or you can see the "Slide Show" on a blank screen as it would be if you were presenting to an audience.

1. Play the animation.

    a. Click on the Play button at the bottom of the Custom Animation Pane.

    b. The animation appears quickly on the slide in the middle pane where you have been working on it. It runs through each action automatically. No mouse clicks are required. This is a quick "rough draft" showing how the animation will work.

2. Run the Slide Show.

    a. Click on the Slide Show button at the bottom of the Custom Animation Pane.

§3.4

b. The screen display changes from the Normal View (with a central pane displaying the slide) to the Slide Show View in which the entire screen is filled with the slide. This is the way the slide would appear if you projected it onto a large monitor or projection screen in a courtroom. The first thing to appear with this slide is its background. The screen should be filled with the background color and nothing else.

c. Click with the left mouse button. The first item in the animation should appear, which is the title box complete with title.

d. Click again with the left mouse button. The second item in the animation should appear which is the blank bullet box.

e. Click again with the left mouse button. The third item in the animation should appear, which is the first bullet point. It should roll across the screen in a Wipe From Left action.

f. Subsequent clicks will bring the rest of the bullet items to the screen.

g. **Right** click when you are finished. This will bring a drop-down menu to the screen.

h. Click on the End Show option. This will take you back from the Slide Show View to the Normal View.

E. Make changes in the animation, if necessary.

As you look at the preview, you may decide to make some changes. The process of making changes is very easy and encourages experimentation. In this case, you might decide to make three changes to the basic animation for the bullet box—

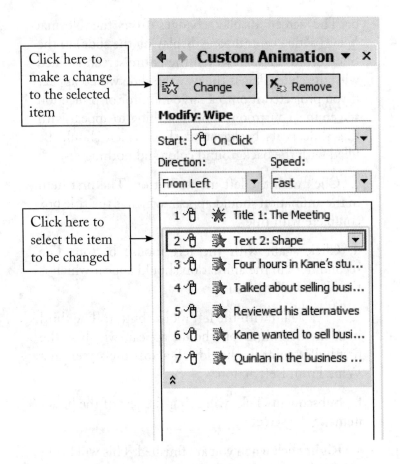

Click here to make a change to the selected item

Click here to select the item to be changed

- Make the bullet box itself "appear" on the screen rather than "wipe from left to right." The bullet box sets the stage for the bullets and usually looks better if it arrives on the screen without motion. If the bullet box has fill color, you can animate it separately (and differently) from the bullet points.

- Make the blank bullet box appear at the same time as the title. Having the bullet box appear by itself when it is empty is somewhat awkward.

- Make each bullet point "dim" as you move on to the next point. When a bullet point "dims," it changes color in a way that moves it to the background. This helps the reader stay focused on the current point, which is in the foreground.

These changes illustrate the basic choices—to change the animation itself (from "Wipe" to something else); to adjust the start control for an animation (having the empty box start with the title); and to add features within an animation (add the "dim" feature along with the Wipe From Left animation).

1. Change the Entrance effect for the underlying bullet box.

   a. Go to the Custom Animation Pane.

   b. Click on the item you want to change. In this case it is the item labeled "Text 2: Shape." That label means that this item is a text box, it was the second item added to the slide, and it is a shape (rather than text).

   c. Note the screen changes. When you click on the item, it will be highlighted with a blue border and a small arrow will appear to the right of the name. The "Effect" button at the top is now called "Change." The name of the current Effect, which is "Wipe" will appear just below the Change button.

   d. Click on the Change button. A menu will appear listing the four types of effects: Entrance, Emphasis, Exit, and Motion Path.

   e. Click on the Entrance option. Another menu will appear listing the Entrance effects.

   f. Click on the Appear option. The underlying bullet box (the rectangular shape in which the bullets appear) will now come onto the screen "in place" with the first mouse click after the title appears.

The Custom Animation Pane now looks like the illustration on page 94.

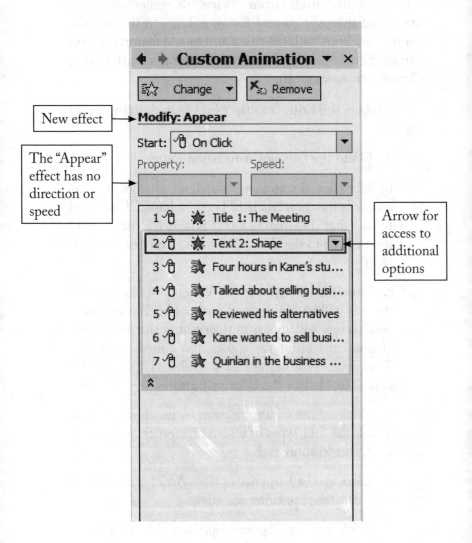

New effect

Modify: Appear

The "Appear" effect has no direction or speed

Arrow for access to additional options

2. Adjust the Start control so that the empty bullet box appears with the title.

    a. Go to the Custom Animation pane.

    b. Click on the listing that represents the bullet box itself. (In the illustration above, it is labeled "Text 2: Shape.") This will activate the listing and a blue border will appear around it together with a small down arrow to its right.

    c. Click on the down arrow to the right of this listing. This will display a list of options.

    d. Click on the Start With Previous option. This will bring the blank bullet box to the screen at the same time as the title box, without any separate mouse click.

Alternatively, you can make the empty bullet box appear with the title by clicking on the access arrow to the right of the listing. Click on Effect Options. Click on the Text Animation tab. Remove the check mark in the front of the option that says "Animate attached shape." (If a check mark is there, click on it to remove it.)

3. Dim each bullet point as you move to the next one.

Dimming bullet points is very useful in a litigation context. It keeps the points on the screen, but in a lighter shade so that the viewer's focus is on the current point. Normally, dimming is used where the explanation of succeeding points lasts more than a minute or two. Bullet points that support very short explanations do not need to be dimmed.

    a. Go to the Custom Animation Pane.

    b. Activate the listing for each bullet point to which the "dim" feature is to be added. Click on the listing to activate it, and a blue border will appear along with an access arrow to the right.

c. Add the "dim" feature to the bullet point.

i. Click on the access arrow to the immediate right of the listing for the bullet point to be dimmed. A drop-down menu will appear.

ii. Click on Effect Options. A dialog box will appear.

iii. Click on the Effect tab at the top of the dialog box. The display looks like this:

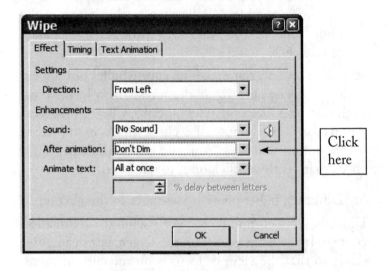

iv. Go to the "The "After animation" box; it should say "Don't Dim." This option keeps the bullet point on the screen without any change. It is the software's default choice.

v. Click on the small down arrow immediately to the right of the box. Another dialog box will appear.

§3.4

This dialog box asks what color you want to use to "dim" the bullet point. Gray is a good color for the "dim" version no matter what color you have selected for the type.

vi. Click on an appropriate color for the bullet point text when it is "dimmed." The dialog box now has the color you picked in the box.

vii. Click on the OK button at the bottom of the dialog box. The "dim" effect has been added, and the AutoPreview will run showing you how the text will look. After running the preview, it snaps back to the draft slide (which will have black text).

4.   Preview your work. Use the method described in step D above to check the changes you have made.

F.   Save your work.

Chapter 4: Photo Slides as Trial Exhibits

Photos are often very important exhibits, but using them effectively in the courtroom presents challenges. When a photo is handed from one juror to another, their collective attention is scattered. Even on an 8-x-10" enlargement, it may be difficult to see relevant details. PowerPoint makes it easy to display any photo on a large courtroom monitor or projection screen. This emphasizes the importance of the exhibit and allows you to talk about particular details while having everyone's attention focused at the same spot.

This chapter covers enlarged photos, cropped and labeled photos, and animation for photo slides.

When working with PowerPoint slides involving photos, you need to keep an eye out for how your work product will be used in the courtroom—whether you intend to introduce it as evidence or use it as an illustrative aid.

The dividing line between evidentiary exhibits and illustrative aids depends on local rules and practice. Some courts will allow a labeled photo into evidence. Other courts will allow the photo into evidence, so long as it has a sufficient foundation, but will require a labeled version of the photo to be treated as an illustrative aid. The usual practical consequence is that evidentiary exhibits can go to the jury room when the jury retires to deliberate, but illustrative aids cannot.

4.1   Evidentiary exhibits—enlarged photos

This section deals with exhibits that are intended to be (or have been) admitted in evidence. Once a sufficient foundation is laid, and the exhibit is admitted in evidence, it can be shown electronically in any way the court determines promotes a fair trial.

Photo slides that are intended to be evidentiary exhibits are drawn from two sources—digital files already on hand and paper copies that must be converted into digital form. This section deals only with digital files. For a detailed explanation of how to deal with photos that are in paper format, see *PowerPoint 2002 for Litigators* (NITA 2002).

Photos used for litigation slides are usually in a format known as JPEG (pronounced jay-peg). This format produces a relatively small file size and is the easiest for courtroom work because the slides containing the photos come to the screen very quickly. Very large files load more slowly, so there is a period of waiting between the time you press the control to move to the next slide and the time the next slide appears on the screen.

A digital photo is available on the NITA Web site, www.nitastudent.org, that can be downloaded and used to construct the slide illustrated in this chapter.

A. Construct a blank slide to hold the photo. (Formatting Toolbar, New Slide button, Slide Layout Pane, Blank Presentation option. See section 2.1.)

B. Import the photo.

1. Go to the Picture Toolbar.

If the Picture Toolbar is not in place, restore it by going to the right of the Drawing Toolbar at the bottom of the screen. (See section 1.4.)

 2. Click on the Insert Picture button. A dialog box will appear. Its display depends on how your computer has been set up and what operating system you are using.

If you are using Windows XP, it will look something like the illustration below. PowerPoint usually goes to the My Pictures folder as its default setting.

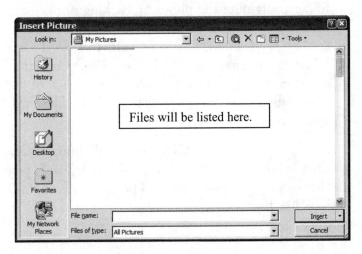

Both types of display work in essentially the same way. They help you by displaying file names so you can click on the one you want.

3. Open the folder where the photo is located. Click on the small down arrow to the right of the "Look in" box as shown in the enlargement below.

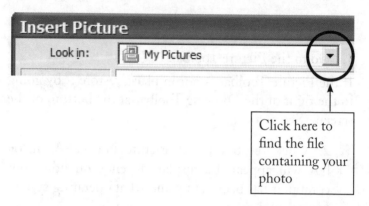

Click here to find the file containing your photo

The photo you want may be on the hard drive of your computer, on a CD, or even on a Web site.

a. If the photo is on your computer, identify the folder containing the photo by clicking on it. (See instructions in section 2.6 for creating a folder to contain slide shows. The same method is used for a folder to contain photos.) Click on the Open button at the lower-right corner. Thumbnails of each of the photos in the folder (or a listing of the files) will appear in the dialog box.

b. If the photo is on a CD, put the CD into the CD drive on your computer. Identify the folder, and open the folder as discussed above. The screen display will look like this.

§4.1

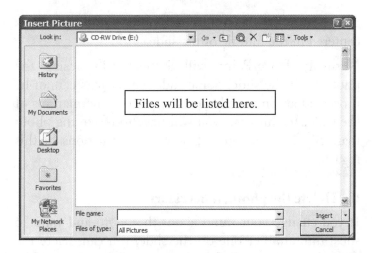

4. Identify the photo you want.

Click on the thumbnail of the photo (or file name for the file containing the photo) to be put on the slide. A blue border will appear around the photo and its file name will be highlighted.

5. Click on the Insert button in the lower-right corner of the dialog box. The photo will appear on the slide. The slide now looks like this.

The photo has been inserted onto the slide and is centered in the middle of the slide.

Normally PowerPoint will automatically resize the photo to fit the slide. Some slide file formats cannot be processed automatically and may exceed the margins of the slide. In this case, you will have to resize the photo manually. See section E below for instructions in this regard.

C. Delete the photo, if necessary.

If you change your mind about the photo and want to substitute another one on the slide, you can delete the first photo. Activate the photo by clicking on it (the border and handles will be showing), and press the DELETE key on the keyboard.

D. Rotate the photo, if necessary.

Occasionally someone has taken a photo with a digital camera that was turned 90 degrees to frame the photo in a particular way. In this case, the digital file will faithfully reproduce the camera angle and the photo will appear sideways when you import it. To turn the photo right side up—

1. Activate the photo by clicking on it.

2. Go to the Picture Toolbar.

 3. Click on the Rotate button. The photo will turn 90 degrees to the left. If more rotation is required, click on the Rotate button again.

E. Resize and move the photo.

Normally an evidentiary exhibit being displayed in enlarged format is centered on the slide as shown above, and PowerPoint places the photo in that location automatically as it imports the photo. However, occasionally an imported photo turns up somewhere else on the slide or in the wrong size for the purpose at hand (usually because of the file format in which the photo was saved) or you need to resize and move the photo in order to put something else on the slide with it.

1. To resize the photo—

    a. Activate the photo. (Move the mouse pointer anywhere within the photo and click once.)

    b. **Right** click on the mouse button. A drop-down menu will appear.

    c. Click on the Format Picture option. A dialog box will appear.

    d. Click on the Size tab. A new display will appear in the dialog box. It looks like this.

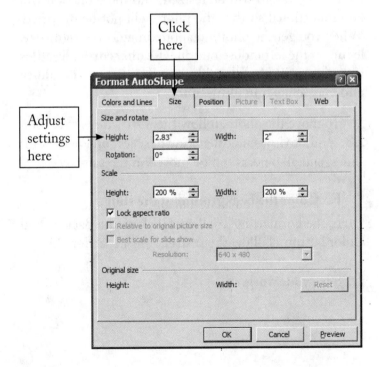

The dialog box contains controls for both height and width.

e. Enter the height that you want. Height is usually the easiest variable with which to work.

f. Check the box that is labeled "Lock aspect ratio." This will change the width proportionately to the change in height and avoid distortion.

g. Click on the OK button at the bottom of the box.

Alternatively, move the mouse pointer over the handle on one of the corners. The mouse pointer shape will change to a two-point arrow. (See illustration at section 1.5.) Hold down the left mouse button. Drag the handle on a diagonal path toward the center to make the photo smaller or away from the center to make the photo larger. The photo will be resized, and the reduction will be proportional so that the photo will not be distorted. When you get the photo to approximately the right size, let up on the left mouse button. **Use only corner handles to resize a photo. The side handles distort the photo and may make it inadmissible.**

2. To move the photo, follow the instructions in section 2.3. A photo is just another kind of object on PowerPoint slides, and all objects can be moved in the same way

 F. Color the background of the slide.

Go to the Formatting Toolbar. Click on the Background Color button. Follow the instructions in section 2.2.

G. Save your work.

4.2 Illustrative aids—cropped and labeled photos

The meaning of a photo may not be clear to the fact-finder without labels, arrows, and other markings that help focus the fact-finder's attention on aspects relevant to particular issues. PowerPoint provides good tools for these purposes. You can crop, title, and label the photo, point out features with arrows, and put a line border around the photo.

Any of these types of enhancements to a photo may draw an objection if the exhibit is offered in evidence. A safer course usually is to use the slide as an illustrative aid for the purpose of assisting the witness in presenting or explaining the testimony.

A. Crop the photo.

Cropping is a method for eliminating unnecessary portions of photos while maintaining the integrity of the remaining portion of the photo. For example, if a photo includes two people, and only one person is relevant to the purpose of the slide, cropping can be used to excise the portion of the photo in which the other person appears. Cropping allows you to focus on a portion of the photo and then enlarge it for easier viewing.

Cropping involves three steps—first, crop the photo to isolate the part you need; second, resize the cropped portion of the photo so that it works well as an exhibit; and third, make fine adjustments to crop further as necessary.

1. Crop the photo.

    a. Activate the photo to be cropped. Move the mouse pointer over it and click once. The handles will appear.

    b. Go to the Picture Toolbar.

    The Picture Toolbar should be located at the bottom of the screen to the right of the Drawing Toolbar. (Illustration on page 6.) If it is not there, restore it. (See discussion in section 1.4(A)).

 c. Click on the Crop button. The handles will change in shape from round hollow circles to black lines.

    d. Put your mouse pointer over one of the *middle* handles.

    The mouse pointer will change shape. As you move the mouse pointer toward the handle, it will have the same shape as the icon on the Crop button. As you line the mouse pointer up with the handle, the mouse pointer will change to a T-shape. The top of the T will line up with the handle.

e. Hold the mouse button down and "push" the handle in the direction you want to go. The margin of the photo will move along with the mouse pointer. When you reach the point where you want the crop to end, let up on the mouse button.

f. If you overcrop, you can take care of the mistake in one of two ways.

> i. Use the Crop tool to back out. The Crop tool will reverse itself if you drag the handle backwards, and will re-expose portions of the photo that had been cropped off.

> ii. Use the Undo tool. Go to the Standard Toolbar, and click on the Undo button one or more times. That will take you back to your previous move, and you can crop again.

g. Click anywhere outside the photo to turn off the Crop feature.

2. Resize the cropped portion of the photo, as necessary.

Cropping usually reduces the size of the photo to the point where it needs to be enlarged to make an effective slide.

a. Activate the photo by clicking on it.

b. Hold the mouse pointer over a *corner* handle until the two-arrow shape appears.

c. Drag the handle outward, to increase the size of the remaining portion of the photo.

3. Crop and resize further, as necessary. Keep in mind that cropping is done with *middle* handles and resizing is done with *corner* handles.

B. Title the photo.

If you plan to explain particular parts of the photo and to refer to those parts more than once, it is often useful to title the photo so that its identification stays in the fact-finder's mind as long as the photo is in view.

The exhibit label, shown in the upper-right corner of this slide, is explained in section 6.2.

To add a title—

1. With the slide containing the photo on the screen, and the photo resized and moved to a location that will accommodate a title (see discussion in section 3.1 above)—

2. Draw a text box.

   a. Go to the Drawing Toolbar.

   b. Click on the Text Box button.

c. Put the mouse pointer on the slide and drag to draw a text box where the title should go. (See discussion in section 2.3.)

3. Add the text of the title.

a. Type the text of the title in the text box.

 b. Center the text within the text box. (With the dotted border showing, go to the Formatting Toolbar, click on the Center button.)

c. Change the typeface and type size as necessary. Tahoma and Arial are good typefaces for trial work. Titles are generally in a 40-point type size or higher. (See discussion in section 3.3(C).)

 4. Put a border around the title box. (Go to the Drawing Toolbar, click on the Line Style button, select a line size.)

5. Resize the box as necessary. (Activate the box and drag the handle in the middle of the right edge of the box.)

6. Center the box on the slide. Move the box until the top and bottom margins are equal and the side margins are also equal.

a. Make sure the Guides are showing and center the box as explained in section 1.1(F).

b. Use the "small move" controls to make fine adjustments in position. Hold down the CTRL key on the keyboard and press one of the Arrow keys on the keyboard.

7. Add color to the border, fill, and lettering in the box as necessary. (See discussion in section 3.3 (G).)

C. Label the content of the photo.

Particular features of, or persons shown in a photo can be identified with labels so that the jury will not get confused and the record of testimony about the photo will be clear.

With the slide containing the photo on the screen and the photo resized and moved to a location that will accommodate one or more labels (see discussion in section 4.1 above)—

 1. Create a text box for the first label. (Drawing Toolbar, Text Box button. See section 2.3.)

Draw the text box for the label with the largest number of letters. (In this case the label for Quinlan would come first, as her name is longer than Kane's.)

2. Put the text of the label in the box.

a. Type in the text.

 b. Adjust the typeface and type size as necessary. (*Dotted* border, Formatting Toolbar, Increase/Decrease Font Size buttons.)

If there is a title on the slide, the labels should use the same typeface and a smaller type size than the title.

c. Center the text within the text box. (*Dotted* border, Formatting Toolbar, Center button.)

3. Enhance the text box as necessary with color for the fill and lettering (in this example the fill is white and the lettering is black) and with a border. (See discussion in section 3.3.)

4. Create a duplicate text box for the second label. (With the text box active, hold down the CTRL key on the keyboard and press the D key on the keyboard.)

5. Replace the text of the original label with the text of the second label. Highlight the text and type in the new text. The old text will be erased. Because this is a duplicate of the first box, it will have the same typeface, type size, alignment, color, and border.

6. Position the labels on the slide.

In the example on page 113 , both labels are placed at the bottom of the photo, equidistant from the left and right margins of the photo, and only a small distance apart. In order to have the same margins at the top and bottom of the slide, the labels overlap the photo a small amount. To align the two labels across the top—

a. Activate both labels at the same time. (Activate one label by clicking on it; then hold down the SHIFT key on the keyboard and clicking on the second label to activate it.)

b. Go to the Drawing Toolbar.

c. Click on the Draw button. A menu will appear.

d. Click on the Align or Distribute option. Another menu will appear.

e. Click on the Align Top option. The tops of the two labels will line up.

D. Point out features with arrows.

In some cases, there may be something about a photo that is not immediately clear without a directional arrow indicating the precise location, or a bit of testimony or a fact may need to be directed to something shown on the photo.

1. Draw the arrow.

a. Go to the Drawing Toolbar.

b. Click on the Arrow button.

c. Move the mouse pointer to the approximate place on the slide where you want the back end of the arrow to start.

d. Hold down the left mouse button and move the mouse toward the point at which the front end of the arrow should be. When you reach that point, release the mouse button. The arrow will appear on the slide.

2. Adjust the style of the arrow, if necessary.

   a. Activate the arrow.

   b. Go to the Drawing Toolbar.

 c. Click on the Arrow Style button. A drop-down menu will appear.

   d. Select the direction and style for each end of the arrow.

3. Change the thickness of the arrow, if necessary.

   a. Activate the arrow.

   b. Go to the Drawing Toolbar.

 c. Click on the Line Style button. A dialog box will appear. (Illustration in section 3.3(A).)

   d. Click on the thickness that you want for the arrow. The arrow will be changed on the screen.

When putting lines on slides, whether in the body of the slide as an arrow or around the edge of a photo as a border, follow the principle of least visual difference. Use a line of the least thickness that will show up well enough on the screen, when enlarged in the courtroom, to make your point.

4. Change the length of the arrow, if necessary.

a. With the arrow active, and its handles showing at each end—

b. Put the mouse pointer over the handle at the end where you want to lengthen or shorten the arrow. The mouse pointer will change to a two-arrow shape.

c. Hold down the left mouse button. Drag the handle in the direction necessary to lengthen or shorten the arrow.

5. Change the color of the arrow, if necessary.

a. Activate the arrow.

b. Go to the Drawing Toolbar.

 c. Click on the small down arrow immediately to the right of the Line Color button. A dialog box will appear.

d. Select a color by clicking on the small box displaying the color or click on the More Colors button to see a palette with a wider choice. (See illustration in section 3.3.)

In the slide illustration on page 116, the arrow has been colored white so that it will contrast better with the background of the slide and the photo.

6. Move the arrow into position.

a. Activate the arrow so that you can move it. Its handles will be showing at either end.

b. Hold down the mouse button and drag the arrow to the approximate position on the slide.

c.   Rotate the arrow, if necessary so that it is pointing in the right direction.

   i.   Position the mouse pointer over one of the handles on an arrow end.

   ii.   Drag the arrow to the right position.

d. Move the arrow in smaller increments, if necessary.

   i.   *Arrow key move*: Press one of the directional ARROW keys on the keyboard a number of times to move the arrow in the direction you want it to go. With each tap of the ARROW key, the arrow on your slide will move one unit of space.

   ii.   *Pixel move*: Hold down the CTRL key on the keyboard and press one of the directional ARROW keys on the keyboard a number of times. With each tap on the ARROW key, the arrow on your slide will move one pixel (a very small amount).

E. Put a line border around the photo.

1. Click on the photo to activate it.

2. Go to the Drawing Toolbar.

 3. Click on the Line Style button. A dialog box will appear.

4. Click on the thickness of the line for the box (or border) around the photo. The box will appear around the photo on the screen.

 5. Color the line if that is useful. The default color of the line is black. To change the color, go to the Drawing Toolbar, click on the Line Color button. A dialog box will appear. Click on the color you want, or click on the More Colors button for a complete palette of colors.

F. Save your work.

4.3   Animation for photo slides

Photo slides usually have considerable interest for jurors and, while animation can add to photo slides under certain circumstances, in many cases no animation at all is required. If you decide to use animation to make the oral presentation more effective, it is a good idea to keep it to a minimum.

Photo slides that are enlargements of exhibits admitted in evidence might be animated only with simple Entrance effects—such as the "Appear" and "Box In/ Out" effects—and no other effects in order to maintain the simplicity of the photo exhibit. Photo slides that are illustrative aids containing explanatory material about the photo are sometimes animated in slightly more elaborate ways.

For detailed instructions, see section 3.4 on the animation of bulleted lists and section 5.4 on the animation of document slides.

Chapter 5: Document Slides as Trial Exhibits

Documents are a majority of the exhibits in many types of cases. Bare enlargements of documents generally do not work well in a courtroom because dense lines of words and numbers do not display well, even on very large screens. For that reason, most PowerPoint slides that deal with documents are illustrative aids. The underlying document is admitted in evidence, and the PowerPoint slides have added marks, explanations, or excerpts that help put the document into proper context.

This chapter covers the basics: displaying a document on a slide; emphasizing portions of the document with lines, boxes and highlighting; using callouts to focus on content; and applying basic animation.

For more specialized methods of presenting documents, and additional detail for particular types of documents, see *PowerPoint 2002 for Litigators* (NITA 2002).

5.1 Display: enlarging a document on a slide

The layout for the first slide created for a document typically has the document sized to fill most of the slide and centered on the slide. The slide has a gray background, and the document's exhibit number is in the upper-right corner. This slide might be used as the first slide in a series that explains the significance of the information in the document. This first slide orients the jurors to the fact that what is coming is an explanation of something that is recorded on a piece of paper and worthy of their consideration.

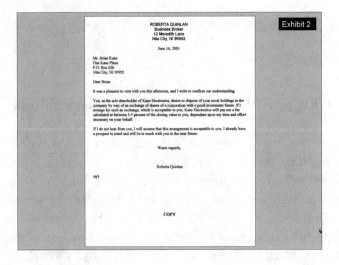

To display a document on a slide, when you already have the document in digital format, you need to construct the blank slide to hold the document, import the document onto the slide, delete or rotate the document if necessary, put a line border around the document, resize and move the document, and add a background color to the slide.

Document slides usually have exhibit number labels in the upper-right corner. See section 6.1 for a discussion of how to construct exhibit labels.

If you have a paper copy of a document and you need to get it into digital format, see *PowerPoint 2002 for Litigators* (NITA 2002).

A sample digital document is available on the NITA Web site, www.nitastudent.com, that can be downloaded and used to construct the slide illustrated in this chapter.

A. Construct a blank slide to hold the document. (Formatting Toolbar, New Slide button, Slide Layout Pane, Blank Presentation option. See section 2.1.)

B. Import the document onto the slide.

The software treats a document like a picture. It is a digital image stored somewhere in a file that needs to be brought onto the slide and used there. Instead of having a separate set of controls for documents, PowerPoint uses the picture controls.

1. Go to the Picture Toolbar.

 2. Click on the Insert Picture button. A dialog box will appear. (Illustration in section 4.1(B).) The dialog box asks for the location of the file that contains the document you want.

3. Enter in the dialog box the location of the document.

Follow the instructions in section 4.1(B).

4. Click on the Insert button in the lower-right corner of the dialog box. The document will appear on your screen.

There is no visible border around the document marking its outer edges, but the handles appear in the corners and in the middle of each edge.

5. If the document is too large for the slide, follow the instructions in section 4.1(E)(1) to get to the right size.

C. Delete a document, if necessary. Activate the document by clicking on it, and press the DELETE key on the keyboard.

 D. Rotate a document, if necessary. (Picture Toolbar, Rotate button.)

Occasionally documents are scanned sideways and, when imported, they will show up sideways on your slide. The Rotate button brings them upright.

E. Put a line border around the document.

In order to make the document look like a page (rather than just text on the screen), you need to put a visible border around it.

1. With the document active, and its handles showing, go to the Drawing Toolbar.

 2. Click on the Line Style button. A dialog box will appear. See illustration in section 3.3(A).

3. Click on the size that you want for the line to be drawn around the document. The line will appear around the edges of the document giving it a low-key border.

For trial slides, it is usually a good idea to use the smallest line that will show up against the background you intend to use. A heavy black line may make the document look somewhat artificial.

F. Resize and move the document.

1. To resize the document so that it occupies as much of the slide area as possible—

a. Move the mouse pointer over a *top-corner* handle. (Resizing with the middle handle will distort the document.) The mouse pointer will turn to a two-arrow shape.

b. Hold down the left mouse button. Drag the handle outward and away from the center of the document. When you get to the size you want, release the mouse button.

2. To move the document to the center of the slide—

a. Move the mouse pointer over the document. The mouse pointer will turn to a four-arrow shape.

b. Hold down the left mouse button. Drag the document to the center. (Alternatively, use the ARROW keys on the keyboard to move the document.)

3. To make fine adjustments to center the document exactly, hold down the CTRL key on the keyboard, and press the ARROW key on the keyboard in the direction the document should be moved.

 G. Add a background color to the slide. (Formatting Toolbar, Background button. See section 2.2.)

The background color should be a medium to light gray or similar color that causes the document to be the center of attention on the slide and does not distract the viewer.

H. Save your work.

5.2 Emphasis: lines, boxes, and circles.

Adding emphasis to a document generally means some form of marking within the four corners of the document to point out its salient features. Sometimes it is a good idea to have more than one slide devoted to a document, and to use different means to get across the essential points about a document. This is better than crowding a single slide with too much information.

A. Lines.

It is occasionally sufficient to merely underline a word or phrase in a document in order to make your point. This usually happens when the point is simply the existence of the word or phrase in the document.

1. Create the line.

   a. With the document on the slide, as shown in section 5.1 above, go to the Drawing Toolbar.

    b. Click on the Line button.

   c. Move your mouse cursor to the place where you want to begin the line.

   d. Hold down the left mouse button and drag the line in the direction you want to go.

When you get to the point where you want to end the line, release the left mouse button.

If you hold down the SHIFT key on the keyboard while you are drawing the line, PowerPoint will know that you want a straight horizontal line or a straight vertical line, and the line will not get off kilter. If you hold the CTRL key on the keyboard while you are drawing the line, PowerPoint will draw the line from the center outward instead of from end to end.

§5.2

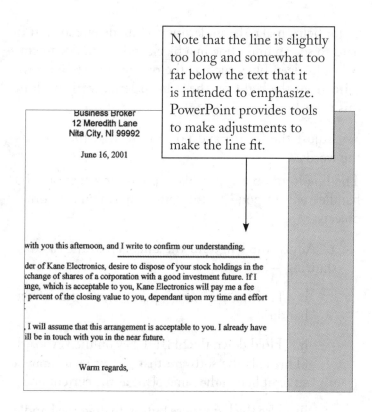

2. Adjust the width and color of the line, if necessary. With the line active, and its handles showing at either end—

 a. To resize, go to the Drawing Toolbar and click on the Line Style button. The default line size will be highlighted. This is usually ¾ point. Click on the line size to be applied.

 b. To color, go to the Drawing Toolbar and click on the small down arrow immediately after the Line Color button. (A dialog box will appear. See illustration in section 3.3(A).) The default color (black) will be highlighted. Click on the color to be applied.

Color helps make the underline technique effective. It is hard to see an underline in a black and white document. A bright deep blue, such as the one on the second row, third from the right on the color palette, works well in this regard.

3. Adjust the length and position so that the line fits the words.

The line is an object, just like a photo or a text box. Its handles will respond to the same adjustments as other objects.

   a. Adjust the length of the line. With the handles showing—

      i. Position the mouse pointer over one of the handles.

      ii. Hold down the SHIFT key on the keyboard. (This tells the software that you want to draw a straight line in the same plane as the current line.)

      iii. Use the left mouse button to drag the handle in the direction of the adjustment you need.

   b. Adjust the position of the line in relationship to the text.

      i. Activate the line so its handles are showing.

      ii. Hold down the CTRL key on the keyboard and press the directional ARROW key on the keyboard (Up, Down, Right, Left). This will move the line in very small increments.

B. Boxes.

The software provides a box that can be put around features of a document, such as the address, the date, or the signature, to emphasize an important point.

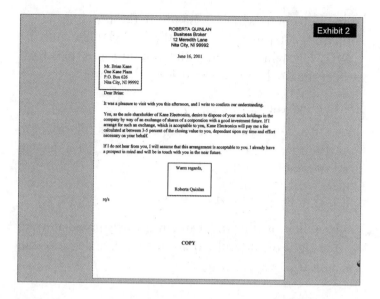

When you want to make a connection between two words or phrases in a document that are not adjacent to one another, you can box or circle them and draw a line between them.

1. Create the box.

    a. With the document on the slide, as shown in section 5.1 above, go to the Drawing Toolbar.

    b. Click on the Rectangle button.

    c. Move your mouse cursor to the place where you want to begin the box.

    d. Hold down the left mouse button and drag the box in the direction you want to go. When you get to the point where you want to end the box, release the left mouse button.

If you hold down the SHIFT key on the keyboard while drawing the box, the box will be perfectly square. If you hold down the CTRL key, the box will be drawn out from the center, which is handy if the box is to cover something. If you hold down the SHIFT key and the CTRL key while drawing the box, the box will be a perfect square drawn outward from the center.

2. Remove the fill.

The software provides a rectangle that has fill, or color, in it. In order for the words to show up on the slide, you need to remove the fill.

    a. Go to the Drawing Toolbar.

     b. Click on the small down arrow immediately to the right of the Fill Color button. A dialog box will appear.

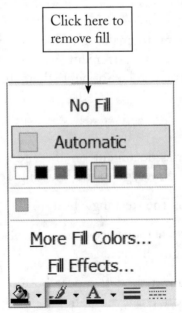

Click here to remove fill

    c. Click on the No Fill button. The color in the box will disappear, and the words will be visible beneath.

3. Change the line width and color.

a. To change the width of the line, go to the Drawing Toolbar and click on the Line Style button. The default line size will be highlighted. This is usually ¾ point. Sometimes a 1½-point line works well. Click on the line size to be applied.

 b. To color, go to the Drawing Toolbar and click on the small down arrow immediately to the right of the Line Color button. The default color (black) will be highlighted. Click on the color to be applied.

A black box does not work well because it does not contrast with the black type. A strong blue is a good choice, such as the color on the second row, third from the right on the color palette.

4. Adjust the position of the box around the words. (*Dotted* border, place mouse pointer over handle, and drag the handle.)

To maintain proportionality while changing the size of the box, hold down the SHIFT key on the keyboard while dragging the handle.

To extend the box from both ends (equally and at the same time), hold down the CTRL key while dragging the handle.

C. Circles.

A circle marks a significant word or set of words in much the same way as a box, although it is less formal than the box. A circle mimics a natural action when a reader circles something on a document using a pen or pencil in order to focus attention on something that is important about the substance of the document.

 A circle added to a document in exactly the same way as a box, using the Oval button on the Drawing Toolbar. The Oval button produces both an oval shape and a circle shape. The circle shows up first and is modified to an oval shape using the handles.

D. Save your work.

5.3   Focus: callouts

Often the best way to make a point about a document is to highlight a phrase or sentence with a callout. This is a method of copying a phrase or sentence from a document, enlarging it, putting it in the margin ("calling it out" of the document) so that it is easier to see, then connecting it to the appropriate point in the original document with one or more line pointers.

This section explains how to make a "rekeyed callout," which is a phrase from the document retyped in a special-purpose box. To do this, you will set up the slide, create the callout box, put text in the callout box and resize it to fit the text, connect the callout box's indicator line, and add colors.

There is also a "direct callout" which enlarges a portion of the text. This type of callout is explained in *PowerPoint 2002 for Litigators* (NITA 2002).

A. Set up the slide.

1. Get the document on the slide as described in section 5.1 above.

2. Move the document to the left half of the slide.

B. Create the callout box.

1. Go to the Drawing Toolbar.

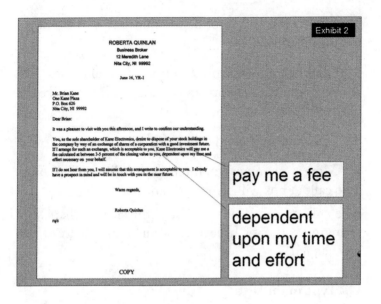

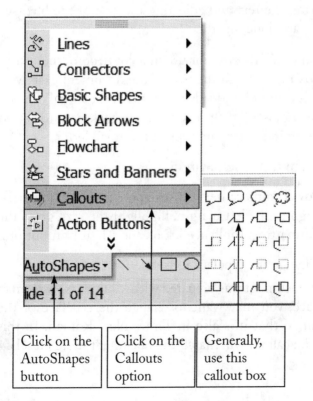

| Click on the AutoShapes button | Click on the Callouts option | Generally, use this callout box |

2. Click on the AutoShapes button. A drop-down menu will appear.

3. Click on the Callouts option. A dialog box will appear containing twenty callout shapes. It looks like the illustration on page 135.

4. Click on the second callout box in the second row.

5. Move your mouse pointer to the slide. Click once. The callout box will be on the slide.

The callout box is not yet the right size or shape, but changing it is easy. It also has a fill color. That can also be changed.

C. Type in the text.

Entering the text and adjusting the size of the box (see below) are done together.

1. Note initial caps. For use in a courtroom, the text in the box must match the text in the document exactly so capitals cannot be added. To get rid of the initial cap, put the cursor just after the capital letter, backspace to get rid of the capital letter, and type in the small letter.

2. Align text to left margin.

 PowerPoint centers all text put in AutoShapes. To align to the left margin, highlight the text, go to the Formatting Toolbar, click on the Align Left button.

3. Change the typeface if useful.

If the document was prepared with a Times New Roman typeface, you may want to change the typeface of the callout so that it is also in Times New Roman. In this way, the callout will match the document more closely.

Document Slides as Trial Exhibits

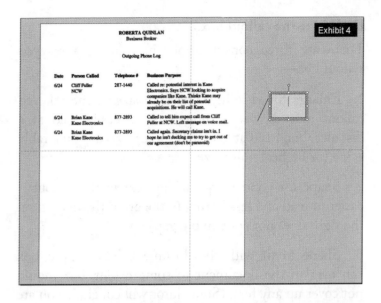

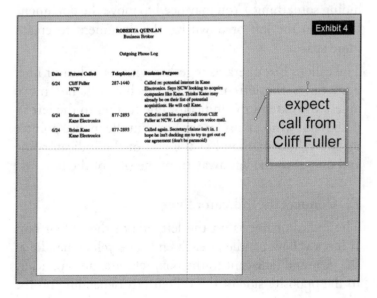

D. Resize the callout box.

There are three considerations in resizing a rekeyed callout box—

1. Enlarge for visibility. The type size in the rekeyed callout must be large enough to be easily read at a distance. You need at least a 32-point size and preferably a 36- (or higher) point size.

2. Shape for good margins. The text in the callout is easier to read and less jarring to the eye if the margin on the right does not contain big gaps.

3. Shape to fit with the document. The callout box can overlap the document to some extent, but should not cover up any text. (Some juror will conclude you are hiding something.) You may need to move the document farther to the left or downsize the document to create more space.

The callout box operates together with its indicator line. Sometimes the left margin of the box will not move unless you extend the indicator line further to the left so it does not wind up under the box. Put the mouse pointer on the yellow diamond at the end of the indicator line and drag it to the left away from the side of the box.

E. Connect the indicator line.

The indicator line is on the left side of the callout box. It has a yellow handle at each end. The yellow handle at the near end (adjacent to the box) relocates automatically to the opposite side of the callout box depending on the direction the line must go. The yellow handle at the far end can be used to stretch and adjust the position of the line. Move the indicator line so that its far end is pointed just above or just below the beginning of the text in the document that corresponds to the text in the callout box.

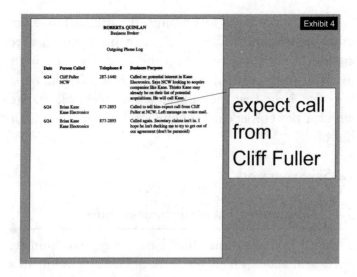

F. Add colors, if useful.

 1. Add background color to the slide. (Formatting Toolbar, Background button.)

2. Change the fill color of the callout box. Like other shapes, the callout box has a colored fill when it is placed on the slide. Sometimes it is effective to make the fill color white and the lettering black because this mimics the document itself.

    a. Go to the Drawing Toolbar.

 b. Click on the small down arrow immediately to the right of the Fill Color button. A dialog box will appear.

    c. Click on the small box displaying the white color.

Alternatively, use a black fill and white letters for emphasis.

3. Change the line color around the callout box. Like other shapes, the callout box has a black line border around it when it is placed on the slide. You may want to change this color, although black is usually the most effective. Note that the indicator line color will change with the box border color. (Drawing Toolbar, Line Color button.)

G. Save your work.

5.4 Basic animation for document slides

This section explains the basic ways to animate document slides. Documents are often key exhibits in a case, and it is important that animation not distract the jury from the facts that the document contains. For this reason, relatively few animation effects are appropriate for regular document slides used in opening statements and direct examination.

Argument slides that use documents for cross-examination or closing argument may have more animation and may use different effects. See *PowerPoint 2002 for Litigators* (NITA 2002).

The method used for applying animation effects to litigation slides is the same regardless of the design of the slide. First, set up to add animations. Then work with Entrance effects—select the effects you want, specify how each effect will work, determine the order in which the effects will be seen on the screen, and then adjust for effects that should run simultaneously.

After you finish with the Entrance effects, use the same sequence to deal with Emphasis, Motion Path, and Exit effects, as necessary. When all the effects have been added, preview the animation and make changes as necessary.

Some document slides work well with no animation at all, and that option should always be considered.

For purposes of this discussion of animation, assume that the document slide looks like this.

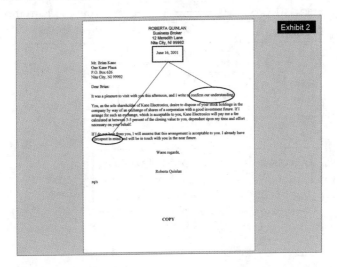

In this slide, the lawyer has illustrated two things in the body of the letter and linked them to the date of the letter. The circles on this slide are constructed in the same way as boxes (the circle button is next to the rectangle button) and the lines are drawn in the same way as explained in section 5.2(A). The exhibit number for the document is in the upper-right corner of the slide. (See section 6.2.)

A. Set up to add animations.

1. Put the document slide on the screen.

   a. Go to the Slides Pane on the left side of the screen.

   b. Find the thumbnail of the document slide and click on it. This will activate the document slide, and it will appear on the screen.

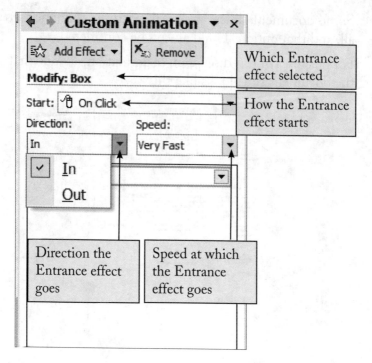

2. Display the Custom Animation Pane on the right side of the screen.

    a. Go to the Menu Bar.

    b. Click on the Slide Show button. A drop-down menu will appear.

    c. Click on the Custom Animation option. The Custom Animation Pane will appear.

B. Select the Entrance effect.

This slide has seven objects on it—a document, an exhibit number label, two circles, two lines, and a box.

1. Activate the first object to be animated (usually the document) by clicking on it. Its handles should be showing.

2. Go to the Custom Animation Pane.

3. Click on the Add Effect button at the top of the pane. A small menu will appear listing the four categories of effects. (Illustration in section 3.4(B).)

4. Click on the Entrance option. Another menu will appear listing the first group of Entrance effects—usually five to nine of them.

5. If the option you want is on the menu, click on it. Otherwise, click on the More Effects button to display a menu listing all of the available effects.

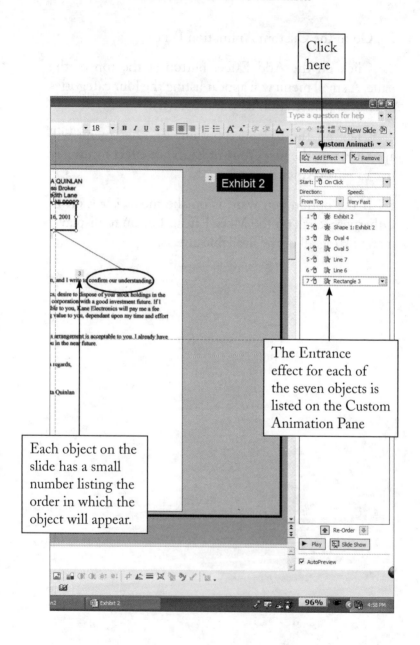

Click here

The Entrance effect for each of the seven objects is listed on the Custom Animation Pane

Each object on the slide has a small number listing the order in which the object will appear.

6. For the document, click on the Box option. The Custom Animation Pane now shows the choice of the Box option. It looks like the illustration on page 142.

7. Activate each object in turn (the exhibit label, the two circles, the rectangle, and the two lines), and complete (2), (3), (4), (5), and (6) above for each object.

The following effects are suggested—

Document	Box, Out, Fast
Exhibit number label	Appear
Two circles	Wipe, From Left, Fast
Rectangle	Wipe, From Top, Fast
Two lines	Wipe, From Bottom, Medium

There are fifty-two Entrance effects. Only a few—such as "Appear," "Box," and "Wipe" are appropriate for document exhibits.

When you finish with these Entrance effects, the screen will look like the illustration on page 146.

C. Specify how the Entrance effect will work.

For most effects, the software provides three variables: how the start-up of the Entrance effect is controlled; the direction from which it enters; and the speed at which it moves as it enters. All three variables are specified using the small boxes at the top of the Custom Animation pane.

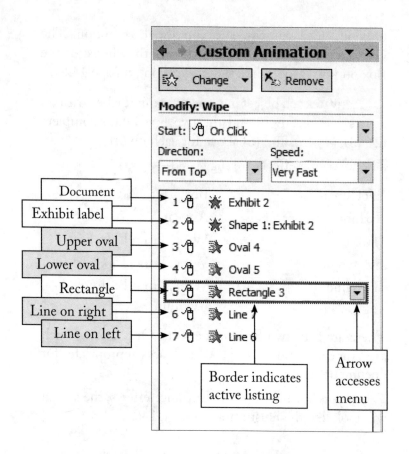

1. *Start*: Check the way the Entrance effect starts. The default choice for the Box effect is "On Click" which means that the Box effect will start when you press the mouse button. Lawyers usually want to control the action on the screen, so this option works well, and no change is needed.

(If you wanted to change the "On Click" option, you would click on the small down arrow to the right of the Start box to see the other choices.)

2. *Direction*: Check the way the Entrance effect moves when the document is brought onto the screen. The default choice for the Box option is "In." Change this to "Out" which works better for documents.

    a. Go to the Direction box. It says "In."

    b. Click on the small arrow to the right of the box. It will display the options for direction with the Box effect. This is shown on the previous illustration. The options are "In" (which is checked) and "Out" (which is not checked).

    c. Click on the "Out" option. A check mark will appear in the checkbox.

3. *Speed*: Check the speed at which the Entrance effect moves when the document is brought onto the screen. The default choice for the Box effect is "Very Fast." This is a little too fast for documents, so change it by clicking on the small down arrow to the right of the Speed box to see the other choices. Select the "Fast" option.

D. Determine the order of the Entrance effects.

The Entrance effects can be moved up and down in the order listed on the Custom Animation Pane. The order depends in large part on the oral presentation that will accompany the slide. In this case—

1. The document is the most important object, so it might come first. That is the order it is currently in.

2. The exhibit number label would logically come next to help keep the identification of the document in the forefront.

3. If the lawyer planned to talk about the phrase "confirm our understanding," the upper oval would come third.

4. If the lawyer planned to talk about the phrase "a prospect in mind," the lower oval would follow the upper oval.

5. If the point to be made is that both of these facts were in existence on June 16, 2001, the date of the letter, the rectangle around the date would come next. The rectangle is currently in the seventh (last) position, so you need to move it up so that it appears immediately after the ovals (and before the lines). To do this—

a. Activate the entry (number 7) on the Custom Animation Pane that represents the rectangle by clicking on it. A blue border will appear around it.

b. Go to the Re-Order Arrows at the bottom of the Custom Animation Pane.

c. Click on the Up Arrow. This will move the Rectangle animation up one notch (above Line 6). Click on the Up Arrow again to move the Rectangle up past Line 5. Now the Rectangle will be animated before the two lines.

The Custom Animation Pane looks like the illustration on page 146.

E. Adjust for Entrance effects that should run simultaneously.

In the illustration on page 146, each animation runs independently on a mouse click. (Every listing has a small mouse icon in front of it.) The motion on the screen would be more seamless if the two lines appeared at the same time, stretching from the ovals up toward the rectangle. In order to have both lines move together, Line 6 needs to start with Line 7.

To do this—

1. Activate the listing on the Custom Animation Pane for the last line. (In the illustration on page 146, that is Line 6.) The listing will have a blue border when it is active. The top part of the Custom Animation Pane will show the animation for this item: the lines are set to Wipe, From Bottom, so that they will go from the ovals up to the rectangle.

2. Click on the small down arrow to the right of the listing. A small drop-down menu will appear.

3. Click on the Start With Previous option. This function will start the animation on Line 6 at the same time as the immediately previous animation which, in the illustration, is Line 7. Both lines will move together. (The mouse click icon that was in front of Line 6 is now gone, indicating that it will move with the mouse click for the listing above it.)

F. Delete an animation, if necessary.

Click on the listing for the particular animation on the Custom Animation Pane (a blue border will be showing), and click on the Remove button at the top of the pane.

G. Select the Emphasis, Motion Path, and Exit effects, if any.

Emphasis effects operate once an object is on the screen. They are "in place" effects that cause the object to be highlighted on the slide.

Motion Path effects move the object from place to place on the screen.

Exit effects take an object off the slide while the slide remains on the screen.

These more advanced effects are not often used with documents. They are described in detail in *PowerPoint 2002 for Litigators* (NITA 2002).

H. Preview the effects.

1. Click on the Slide Show button at the bottom of the Custom Animation Pane. The background of the slide will appear on the screen.

2. Click the mouse button to go through the animations. Each object will appear at a click.

3. Right click at the end. A small menu will appear.

4. Click on the End Show option. This will take you back to the Normal View.

I. Make changes as necessary.

If the preview shows that the animation should be changed, perhaps to a different Entrance effect, do this—

1. Go back to the Custom Animation Pane.

2. Click on the listing for the object that has the animation you want to change. The listing will be highlighted with a blue border. The "Add Effect" button at the top of the pane will now be a "Change" button.

3. Click on the Change button at the top of the pane. A small menu will appear listing the four types of effects.

4. Click on the Entrance option. A menu will appear listing the Entrance effects.

5. Click on your new choice for the Entrance effect.

6. Click on the Start, Direction, and Speed attributes for the new Entrance effect, if necessary.

J. Save your work.

Chapter 6: Exhibit Labels and Slide Numbers

Evidentiary exhibits have an exhibit number label, usually in the upper-right corner of the slide. It is useful to put the exhibit number in the same place on every slide as it helps jurors become familiar with the evidentiary material more quickly.

Illustrative aids that incorporate exhibits like documents or photos usually display the exhibit number of the document or photo for persuasive purposes. However, the court may require that every exhibit shown to the jury during trial have a separate number. Under those circumstances, the illustrative aid itself will have an entirely separate exhibit number.

PowerPoint has an automated capability to add slide numbers, which may be useful for keeping track of the presentation in your trial notes.

6.1   Exhibit labels

Exhibit number labels should be of the same size, in the same location, and in the same format on all slides that use evidentiary material. Examples of slides with exhibit number labels are on pages, 112, 113, 124, and 135.

Once an exhibit label format is created for a slide, it can be copied to all subsequent slides. The format of the exhibit label, including its position in the upper-right corner of the slide, will be carried over to the new slide.

A. Create a text box to contain the exhibit number. (Drawing Toolbar, Text Box button. See section 2.3.)

B. Type the exhibit number.

Change the typeface and type size if necessary. (See section 4.2.) Tahoma and Arial are useful typefaces for trial work. An 18-point size is usually sufficient for exhibit number labels.

C. Resize the text box, if necessary. (See section 2.3.) Be sure to create a box that is large enough for any exhibit number (or sub-number, like Exhibit 103a) so that you can use the same text box on subsequent slides.

D. Create a distinctive format for the text box.

One fairly standard way to display exhibit labels is white text on a black background. This differentiates the exhibit label from almost all other kinds of things a lawyer might put on a slide.

With the *dotted* border showing on the text box—

 1. Change the color of the type to white. (Drawing Toolbar, Font Color button, white option.)

 2. Change the color of the fill to black. (Drawing Toolbar, Fill Color button, black option.)

E. Position the box in the upper-right corner of the slide. (See section 2.3.)

The exhibit label looks best if it is in a corner and equidistant from the margins of the slide. If you decide to position the text box in the upper-right corner (which is a standard position), you want to have an equal distance from the top margin and from the right margin.

F. Copy the exhibit number box and paste it on another slide.

1. Activate the original exhibit number box by clicking on it.

2. Hold down the CTRL key on the keyboard and press the C key on the keyboard. This is the command for the software to create a copy. Nothing happens on the screen.

3. Go to the slide where you want to place the copy. (Have this slide on the screen in Normal View.)

4. Hold down the CTRL key on the keyboard and press the V key on the keyboard. This is the command for the software to paste the copy you have created. The exhibit number box will appear in its correct position in the upper-right corner.

5. With the *hatched* border showing, delete the old exhibit number and add the new exhibit number.

6.2 Slide numbers

You may want to put slide numbers on your slides so that you can find them in the slide show when working from hard copies. It may be convenient to have printouts of your slides, and you may want to jump from one point to another in the slide show. If you have slide numbers on the slides, they will also be on the printed copies.

A. Open the Header and Footer dialog box.

1. Go to the Menu Bar.

2. Click on the Insert button. A drop-down menu will appear.

3. Click on the Slide Number option. A dialog box will appear.

4. Click on the Slide tab at the top of the dialog box. The display in the dialog box will look like this.

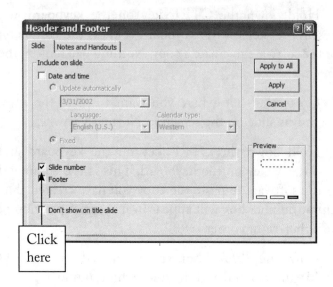

B. Designate slide numbers.

1. Click on the small checkbox in front of the Slide Number option. A check mark will appear in the box.

2. Click on the Apply to All button in the upper-right corner. A small footer has been inserted into each slide that will bear its slide number, as assigned by the system. This will be the same slide number as appears on the Slides Pane or in the Slide Sorter View.

Chapter 7: Showing and Printing Slides.

Slides can be shown or printed at any stage. When you show the slides (either on a computer screen or projector screen), they are displayed full size with none of the working screen components. When you print slides, they can be full size (one to a page) or in thumbnails (more than one to a page).

7.1 Showing slides

PowerPoint has automated most of the features for showing your slides.

A. Open the slide show. (See section 2.7(C) and (D).) The first slide will be on the screen.

B. Open the Slide Show View.

The slide show control is on the View Bar, which is a small toolbar in the lower-left corner of the screen, just above the Drawing Toolbar. It looks like this.

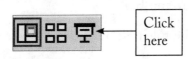

The View Bar's function is to switch among the three "views" available in PowerPoint—the Normal View (which is used to construct slides), the Slide Sorter View (which is used to move slides and add transitions), and the Slide Show View.

The button to switch to the Slide Show View is the last on the right. Click on this button to begin the slide show. The show will begin with whatever slide is on the screen at the time.

C. Use the left mouse button to advance the slide show.

Click the left mouse button once to advance to the next animation or the next slide. (*Alternatively*, use the SPACE BAR on the keyboard.)

D. Use the right mouse button to end the slide show.

To leave the Slide Show View and go back to the Normal View—

1. Click on the right mouse button. A menu will appear.

2. Click on the End Show option. The view will switch back to the Normal View.

7.2 Printing slides

Printing copies of slides is a very straightforward process. All of the necessary controls are in one place.

A. Open the Print dialog box.

1. Go to the Menu Bar.

2. Click on the File button.

3. Click on the Print option. A Print dialog box will appear. It looks like this.

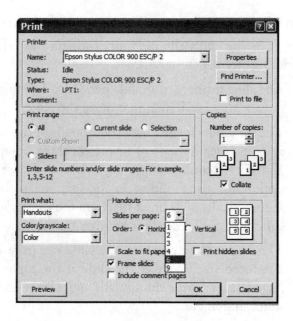

B. Specify how the slides should be printed.

1. What slides do you want to print?

The Print Range area in the middle of the dialog box contains the choices for what should be printed.

- All the slides in the slide show that is currently active.

- The current slide that is active within a slide show.

- Selected slides within the slide show that is currently active. (You can do this in two ways—by highlighting the slide thumbnails, or by designating the slide numbers.)

- A Custom Show. (The box to the right of this option allows you to locate the show that you want to print.)

2. In what format do you want to print the slides?

Slides can be printed in four formats—as slides, handouts, notes pages, or outlines.

- The slide format is one slide per 8½-x-11"-printed page with a small margin around the edges.

- The handouts format uses thumbnails of the slides and provides options of one, two, three, four, six, and nine thumbnails per page. If you choose the option for three slides on a page, the software automatically adds lined spaces to the right of each slide that can be used for handwritten notes.

- The Notes Page provides one slide per page with a reduced size image of the slide at the top of the page (larger than a thumbnail) and a place to type notes underneath.

- The Outline View provides all of the text on the slides in an outline format.

The option to print slides four to a page or six to a page is helpful for trial preparation, as these printouts are used with trial notes so the lawyer knows what slide is coming next.

Slides can be printed in three color options—in color (for color printers), in grayscale (for black and white printers), and in pure black and white (usually not of use in litigation applications).

3. How many copies do you want to print?

The control for the number of copies is a small up-down arrow on the right side of the dialog box.

If you print multiple copies, you can use the "Collate" feature to print in sets. When the Collate checkbox is checked, the printer will print all the pages of set 1, then all the pages of set 2 and so on. If the Collate checkbox is not checked, the printer will print all the copies of page 1, then all the copies of page 2, and so on.

Alternatively, if you have already set all of the controls, go to the Standard Toolbar, click on the Print button. This bypasses the Print dialog box.

C. Select the quality level for the printout.

1. Click on the Properties button in the upper-right corner. A dialog box will appear.

2. Click on the Paper/Quality tab. A dialog box will appear containing the options for paper size and quality. The default setting for quality is not at high resolution, and you may need higher quality for printing slides to use as backup if necessary on an evidence camera or to show your client or others involved in your case, or where you have a detailed slide that will only be clearly visible with higher resolution printout.

Chapter 8: More PowerPoint Features.

More advanced features and wider uses of PowerPoint are described in detail in *PowerPoint 2002 for Litigators* (NITA 2002). This larger book comes with a CD that contains slide shows demonstrating all of the color and animation that cannot be portrayed on a black and white page. It is set in the context of a demonstration case, so that all of the examples are drawn from a cohesive set of exhibits.

In addition to more examples of bullet point, photo, and document slides, this larger book includes:

Diagram, Table, Timeline, and Chart Slides as Trial Exhibits

Place diagrams
Process diagrams
Tables
Timelines
Organization charts
Statistical charts

Argument Slides as Trial Exhibits

Weight of the evidence slides
Relationship charts
Yes-No checklists
Decision tree charts
Relative merit charts
Pushy timelines
Attack slides
Other useful techniques for argument slides

Slides with Video and Audio Elements

> Slides with video clips
> Slides with audio clips

Slides with Presentation Features

> Transitions
> Hidden slides
> Custom Show
> Hyperlinkiing

Collaborating with Colleagues on Slides

> Notes on slides
> Comments on slides
> Copying slides to or from another slide show
> Delivering printed copies of slides
> Delivering digital copies of slides
> Collaborating using the Web

Setting Up a Computer for Using Slides at Trial

> Make a digital backup copy
> Match resolution
> Optimize the slide show
> Turn off the standby timer
> Set toggle switch position
> Set audio switch position
> Clean up the computer's ancillary displays

For sales, contact the NITA Web site, www.nita.com, or call 1-800-225-NITA.